D1627118

The Missing Mentor

*Women Advising Women on Power,
Progress and Priorities*

By

Mary E. Stutts

Household
Publishing

Atlanta

Household
Publishing

A Division of Household Publishing and Enterprises, Inc.
4355 Cobb Parkway, Suite J287
Atlanta, Georgia 30339

For information about special discounts for bulk purchases to be used for corporate training programs, seminars, and workshops, please contact Household Publishing Sales Department: 678-872-4504

COVER DESIGNED BY CAROLINA WHEELER

INTERIOR DESIGN AND LAYOUT BY REGINALD TOLBERT

www.h2opublishers.com

Printed in the United States of America

First Edition: May 2010

10 9 8 7 6 5 4 3 2 1

Library of Congress Cataloging-in-Publication Data

ISBN 978-0-9772730-9-6

Business – Management
Mary E. Stutts

Acknowledgements

So many people have made this book possible that I don't have the space to thank them all. This includes my family, friends, colleagues, professors and coaches from over the years.

I especially want to acknowledge the wonderful women who so graciously added their experiences to mine to answer some of the many questions women have about career and life choices.

For more information:

http://www.themissingmentor.com

The female mentoring market needs a spokesperson to educate them on issues that affect them everyday. *The Missing Mentor: Women Advising Women on Power, Progress and Priorities* will serve as a valuable tool in your arsenal of personal and career preparation and provides real life anecdotes and professional advice to help you progress and prioritize. Examples of real life situations are presented and the recommendations are applied to women that need mentoring in each chapter.

*The Missing Mentor: Women Advising Women on Power,
Progress and Priorities*

Table of Contents

Foreword

Mary has a real understanding of what it takes for women move into powerful careers. She naturally thinks about how to bolster up someone's authority, standing and confidence in a significant way that is never arrogant or egotistical – that keeps them grounded in their own strength and their own possibilities.

Mary's focus in this book on empowerment and parlaying individual uniqueness to create a career and life path fills a great need for women of all ages, but especially women who are trying to make up their minds about career opportunities, education, marriage, kids and overall direction in life. Many of these women are craving a strong mentor who has actually done it all. Mary has, and her reactions to situations and people are honest and immediate, never planned or contrived. Her language reflects that and only serves to enhance and encourage power in others. This is why Mary's down-to-earth, humorous, elegant and compelling approach, captured and relayed so well in this book, is so well received.

Mary and the powerful, accomplished women profiled in this book cross paths with women from all walks of life and are struck by how many of them are seeking to balance and integrate achieving personal dreams and desires with maintaining relationships in the home, work place, church or community.

This book will serve as a valuable tool in your arsenal of personal and career preparation and provides real life anecdotes and professional advice to help you progress and prioritize.

Myrtle Potter
CEO & Founder, Myrtle Potter Company
Former President and COO, Genentech
CNBC Commentator

Introduction
Power, Progress and Priorities

Looking out over the San Francisco Bay from my office my first day on the job at Genentech in 2001, I was more sad than excited. Already I missed my friends and colleagues on the other side of the Bay at Bayer's Global Biotechnology Business Unit in Berkeley. I had asked myself a lot of questions before taking this new position. Let's see. Do I go or do I stay? Do I take a risk or play it safe? Do I want to stick with the security of a large company with 30,000 employees or take a chance with a smaller company of 4,000 employees and a question mark about its future success? How is this new and twice-as-long commute going to impact my family time? Who can I talk to about this who has faced similar decisions?

Unfortunately for me, at that time, I was not connected to any powerful female mentors. So I had to rely on my gut instincts, lessons learned from my own experience and prayer. I knew that the only promotion for me at Bayer lay in moving to the East Coast or Germany. I did not see that as an option for my family or me. Of course, I could have just stayed where I was. But something inside wouldn't let me do that either, once this opportunity presented itself.

I had learned over the years that, in most instances, I needed to go through the doors that opened for me. Since completing undergraduate school at the University of Louisiana and graduate school at University of Southern California, I had worked for seven companies up to that point in my career. In many instances, the jobs came looking for me. Even as I wrestled with taking this job, I knew instinctively that the more emotional resistance I experienced the greater likelihood that there was something unique about this job and that I needed to hunker down and let whatever that destiny was unfold in my life.

It was a bumpy, emotional ride for me that first year – not because of the great people or company, but because of my own reluctance to accept and embrace the change. It was a new and different culture. From my first day of school at five years old, I prided myself on being an A student in every class and every situation. I carried that same pride of performance to every company I worked for. But everybody at this company was an A student. Most were A+. Not only that, but everyone was expected to maintain that A+ mentality and approach. The first word used to describe a job candidate or new colleague at this company

2

was always, "He or she is very smart."

Eventually, I connected with two very "smart" and powerful women in leadership at Genentech who took it upon themselves not only to befriend me, but to informally mentor and nurture me: Dr. Susan Desmond Hellmann and Myrtle Potter. In fact, my research on them had played a large part in convincing me to accept the offer that I had received from the company.

The next six years were not only a culmination of all the great experience and lessons I had learned in the media, at Kaiser Permanente and Bayer Pharmaceuticals but were also a cultivation of my growth and maturity as a leader. Two years later, when I became the head of my department, one of the most amazing growth phases in the company's history began. We had 15 positive phase-III clinical trials in a row, and revenues increased from $2 billion to $9 billion during the next four years. My department grew from 16 employees and an annual budget of $14 million to 43 employees and an annual budget of $100 million, and new areas of responsibility were added to the scope of my job during that time. Accepting that challenge and embracing the change that went along with it became levers to usher me up to the next levels of leadership in my career.

Since then I have moved on to senior level global positions at Fortune 50 companies in healthcare, media and technology industries. A main attribute of my leadership style is making sure every member of my team – male and female – has a professional development plan that I personally coach them on creating and implementing. Profession development workshops have become a popular component of my 'Missing Mentor' leadership development program.

As you are reading this, you may be asking questions similar to those I asked: Should I go back to school or just rely on work experience? Am I ready for promotion? How can I get out of this rut? Can I really do this? What if I fail? What's my next move? Is my industry growing? Should I focus on job security or more money? Do I want to join a big company or small company? What's the right decision for my family? Can I have it all? Who can I talk to about all of my choices?

At some point in life, everyone asks most (if not all) of these questions. No matter how powerful you are or become, there is always a time of weighing the balance. If you're not asking any of these questions, it may be an indication of a bigger issue, like lack of planning, fear of challenging yourself, or just plain willingness to settle for less than the best.

For 30 years, I have enjoyed an exciting and progressive career that has not been plagued by a lot of the fits and starts I hear so many complain about. That's not to imply that I haven't encountered any surprises, rough patches and disappointments, but I have always maintained consistent, steady progress, initially in print and broadcast media and then for the last 20 years in healthcare.

I have learned a lot over the years, about people, about evaluating opportunities, about making the most out of the chances we are given, about what's really important, about what is lasting and what is fleeting, about how to recognize potential and how to identify and avoid what I call "fatal flaws." I have made some lifelong friendships and built relationships with other women in leadership who have unique stories, paths and approaches as well.

As my career has evolved I am frequently asked to speak at conferences and participate in panels about career advancement, women in leadership and work-life balance. Since I love people and the opportunity to help others learn from my progress and mistakes, doing this work is one of my favorite activities. A regular feature at many of these events is the "Ask Mary" session, where I answer questions about whatever is on the audience members' minds. Inevitably, the questions always turn to mentoring. It is the most popular topic for women seeking to advance, change or jump-start their careers – and with good reason.

A recent article in the Journal of Healthcare Management summarized a 2005 study on strategic thinking.

Being mentored was number one on their list of experiences that lead to the ability to think strategically. The article concludes that mentoring should occur in the first few years of one's career and include frequent contact (weekly, preferably) between the mentor and the protégé to be contributory to strategic thinking. Laurence Merlis, in providing a practitioner application of the study, adds that mentoring's optimal use should not be limited to early careerists. Mentoring works well for mid-careerists and senior leaders as an effective tool for strategic thinking too. (I provide more perspective on the significance of strategic thinking in career advancement in Chapter One.)

But women frequently lament not being able to find a successful and powerful female mentor. What has become apparent is that few women provide consistent mentoring to other women. Men actually provide more mentoring assistance overall in the workplace.

While there may be a variety of reasons for this, and while women are appreciative of male input, I have consistently heard from women that they crave the advice of women in leadership positions. According to an article by Eleanor Mills in the Feb. 7, 2010, edition of London's The Sunday Times, 60 percent of Europe's and 57 percent of America's college graduates in 2006-07 were women. Not only in the West, but in what is called the BRIC economies - Brazil, Russia, India and China, there is a groundswell of highly educated girls moving through the workplace, says Mills. There is no way women in senior level positions can individually mentor all of these bright and ambitious young women. There are simply not enough female leaders. Therefore, this ever-growing crop of young professional women will have to find alternative ways to get the advice and counsel they seek.

While there is a shortage of senior-level women capable of the mentoring needed, the ones who exist cannot always be counted on to mentor either. One explanation I have heard from these missing mentors themselves is that, no matter how high a woman may have climbed up the career ladder, she is still the main care provider at home. Her duties extend to housework, cooking and chauffeuring! That means she simply does not have the time to provide this level of support, - much to her chagrin.

It is interesting that, to this day, I have never heard a male colleague lament about work- life balance. It is for precisely this reason that women want to get advice and counsel from women in powerful positions who can relate to the challenges they face, not only at work but also at home. I cannot begin to count the number of women who have asked me if I could mentor them one-on-one. While I love mentoring and am a great advocate of many protégés, it is not physically possible for me to accommodate all of the requests I receive. Many women in leadership face this same conflict of desire versus availability.

This book was created by women who desire to help other women navigate a bright career and future. It contains lessons from women advising women on power, progress and priorities.

Whether you are just starting or are in the midst of building a career, you have likely already figured out that it is going to take significant power sources to energize you to maintain your warp speed pace and achieve your highest visions of success. Creating a plan is just the first step. You are going to have to "power up" every day to maintain your focus, make the daily choices you will face and avoid derailing yourself with unforeseen pitfalls. To become gain success and authority, you'll need the right tools to forge your path. Faith, courage, and a continuing thirst for pursuit of knowledge are only the beginning.

And, yes, you probably won't be able to find a mentor available to invest the amount of time you need to answer all of the questions you have. That is why the women profiled in this book have taken the time to answer your questions and offer you advice and counsel in a manner that is down-to-earth, humorous, elegant and compelling.

The Missing Mentor: Women Advising Women on Power, Progress and Priorities is written from my multiple perspectives as a senior executive, mentor, protégé, counselor, wife and mother and is designed to assist you in making wiser choices every day, at home or on the job. The book includes tips, advice and real-life examples of prioritizing and how to derive the power you need to keep moving forward. Each chapter features a "Power Up!" interview with inspiring advice from women who have achieved great things in all walks of life.

Whether you're just starting your career or you've been in the workforce for 30 years, you're concerned about your performance and all of the change going on around you. It may seem like you're stuck in a rut, or as though your life is literally standing still. Or you may feel like you're on a conveyor belt that is moving too fast for you to find the controls. It's not that you don't care about your future – it's much more likely that you desperately want to learn how to stay one step ahead of it. If you can learn to do that, you reason, you'll be able to move, undaunted, toward a much better life. If any of this sounds like you, this book will give you exactly what you need most! It will help you:

- increase you confidence and "presence";
- assess where you've been, and where you're going to be in the future;
- learn how to position yourself well for this time of rapid, endless change;
- become more self-aware than ever;
- recognize choices about your personal and profes-

sional lives;

- sustain your ethics, soul and spiritual wellbeing;
- build and nurture important relationships, both personal and professional;
- envision and create a successful long-term plan for progress
- avoid getting derailed with missteps and missed opportunities

The good news is that success is in your hands. You can gain and maintain control to drive your future. This is your opportunity to shine.

Are you ready now? Let's get "powered up" for the future!

Are you a Woman of Power, Progress and Priorities?

- Do you find change to be a positive experience? Is the future exciting for you?
- Are you always looking for the next big opportunity in your career?
- Are you linked in to future trends, constantly learning about new businesses, jobs or ideas that only existed a few moments before?
- Do you have a development plan designed to increase and enhance your strategic thinking and planning capabilities?

- Are you well connected to the world with technology that not only makes communication easy but also streamlines your life? Do you like to stay ahead of developments in new technology or programs?
- Are you very flexible when it comes to switching gears on a moment's notice?
- Do you already have in place a support network of people who provide you with the things you need to succeed (like mentoring, career coaching, spiritual guidance)?

Are you ready for the constant changes that happen in both your business and personal lives? You need not only to survive, but also to thrive on the concepts of lifelong learning and total self-reinvention. You are always in a state of becoming the person you dreamed of being – even as that dream morphs into another, and another, and another. You are at peace within yourself and with the rest of the world.

If this sounds like where you want to be, read on! There's still time to get back on track for the ride of your life.

Chapter One
Confidence is Power – Using It or Losing It
"Experience tells you what to do; confidence
allows you to do it"
- Stan Smith

The most important thing we can do in life is show up. By that I mean be fully present in the moment as our true powerful selves. Each of us has strength, reserves of it we may not even realize we have, and when we tap into those reserves, we are unstoppable. Our self-assurance commands the attention of others in the best way. We show them who we are, and what we can do. We are, in other words, confident. Those around us observe our poise, which manifests in our behavior, body language, voice, and words, and they listen to us and believe us, because nothing is as compelling as confidence. It is a manifestation of the strength and authority we have. It is, in a word, our power.

When we are self-confident, we inspire others

to have confidence in us. We also show them who they can be and what they can do. An audience will sit on the edge of its seats to hear your next point, ready to implement the advice you give as soon as they leave that conference. Your bosses will pay close attention to your proposal. Your customers will be excited about that new product you promote. Your peers will be inspired by your positive energy and enthusiasm. Gaining the confidence of others is one of the key ways in which a self-confident person finds success. Recognizing your strengths, and the confidence that results from doing that, then, is key to your success both professionally and personally.

Understanding the need for power and confidence, however, does not mean you can automatically produce those aspects of yourself. For some of us, it takes more than knowledge. You may have been an excellent student. You may be more than competent in your job. You have family members who love and believe in you. You may have had some success at your current company. Your boss may like and trust you. But, you know there is something holding you back.

You can do more. You are not all you can be. You are not manifesting the strength that you have. Why not?

Many people struggle to find their confidence. You may never have allowed it to surface, or you may have buried it long ago. Some of you, mainly women, simply gave it away. Why would you do that? Mainly because women tend not to want to ruffle any feathers or rock the boat or…well, you pick the metaphor. The point is women are, generally speaking, peacekeepers. But to be a successful peacekeeper, we often have to keep our opinions to ourselves, modify our ideas, or accept what we are given. All of these things rob you of the strength you need for success. One way to re-capture that power is to recognize those things that have stolen it from you. Things like intimidation, your own politeness, fear, shyness, your lack of education or technological skills may make you feel powerless.

The good news is that there are methods for finding your confidence, or, in some cases, relearning it. There are those around you who will help you claim or reclaim your power and harness it. In my case, that someone came in the form of an executive coach from

Stanford University.

I had recently been placed in an interim position as a Regional Director at Kaiser Permanente, and I knew I had to do a good job in order to snag a permanent position. The information on the Stanford leadership development program had come across my desk and caught my attention. Leadership. Well, wouldn't that be cool, I thought. Certainly it was my intention to move beyond a director-level position and as high up the career ladder as possible. I have always been ambitious, and in those early days, I probably had more ambition than confidence – or knowledge about my industry for that matter, but I was not about to let that stop me. Fortunately, my company approved my request and paid for me to participate in the program.

Settling into my chair at the Stanford class, I took a deep breath of satisfaction. I had made it there. I knew it would help me gain skills I needed to reach that next level of success. The room filled up with more men than women, and from the looks of it, I was among the youngest executives in the room. The instructor strode in and introduced himself as Milo, an abbreviated form of his very long and often misspelled surname - Dr. James Milojkovich. He then forged ahead with his opening comments, the main premise of which was that most people come to the program to hear what to do and how to dress to be a leader. But, Milo stressed the point that leading is a way of being, rather than a bullet-pointed checklist. So far, so good, I thought. Milo and I were on the same page.

Before we moved on to the first exercise of the day, we 20 students introduced ourselves. Members of the class included a police chief for a large metropolitan district, and a female executive who was the CEO of a regional airline. She had formed the airline with a partner and various senior executives from companies including Hewlett Packard, Sun Microsystems, Intel, Cisco Systems, Oracle and Apple. My classmates were an impressive group to say the least.

Following introductions, Milo moved us into the first exercise of the day. He asked class members to volunteer to stand before the class to tell why they entered the program. The police chief raised his hand and went up to speak first. I thought he did a pretty good job. He received some critiquing on his presentation style and sat down. Well, that wasn't so bad I thought. I raised my hand and was invited to come up.

I launched into my best "on stage" persona and talked about my frustration surrounding my job and its current focus. I was tired of doing the same thing and was ready for a change. I explained that I wanted to move into a different career path and do more challenging work. I smiled sweetly at the professor and my very cordial and attentive classmates, waiting for what I and everyone else assumed would be a nice critique like the one before.

"Thank you Mary. Did you give a lot of speeches when you were a kid?" Milo asked.

"Yes," I replied. My foster father was a minister, so my siblings and I had to give speeches and say poems all the time.

"Yes, and did you bounce and do little pirouettes and courtesies?" Milo continued.

It began to dawn on me that this was not heading in the right direction. Where is a good earthquake when you need one, I thought, as I wished the floor would just swallow me up. I could sense my class-mates' jaws dropping as well.

"That was the nice Mary who wants to please ev-erybody," Milo informed me and the class. "Now I want the real Mary to tell me why she's here, and I want her speak as though people can take it or leave it."

I followed his advice and did it again, this time voicing my real feelings and convictions. I moved around on the stage as I spoke, looked people in the eye to make sure I was connecting and did not focus on smiling so much.

"Now wasn't that a more powerful Mary?" Milo asked the class when I finished. Everyone nodded enthusiastically in agreement. I went to my seat (okay, with my chest stuck out just a little bit).

But Milo wasn't finished with me yet. "Initially Mary was not convincing. Her movement was con-strained. She was being a passive aggressive people-pleaser, worrying about what people would think," he explained.

In case you're wondering how the exercise end-ed, I was followed by two of the technology executives, then the airline executive raised her hand and another male executive. After about six people presented, Milo announced he was ending the opportunity to volunteer. He announced to the rest of the class that those who didn't raise their hands were not leaders. True leaders are not afraid to learn in front of others.

I have since earned a certificate in a more intensive global leadership program at Stanford's business school and have completed leadership programs at various companies where I've gone on to work, but I credit this initial class with opening my eyes to the significance of confidence, my presence and how I "show up" in whatever I'm doing.

Coaching Confidence

Several free follow-up coaching sessions with Milo were included as part of that initial leadership program. Following my tenure at Kaiser, I joined Bayer and brought Milo in as a leadership speaker there. A few years later, when I was promoted to run my department at Genentech, Milo became my personal coach as part of my development plan. He continues to work with me today.

If your company offers development support and the opportunity to work with a personal coach, I encourage you strongly to please take advantage of it. You should never underestimate the value of having an objective, knowledgeable observer provide feedback on how you show up, work, think and speak. Having a trusted third party to bounce ideas off of as you're managing your staff and workload and staying out of the weeds can be invaluable.

If your company does not offer the option of working with a personal coach, there are many organizations out there from which you may choose if you decide to find one on your own. The field of personal and professional coaching has grown substantially over the past 10 years, according to Carter Mc-Namara, MBA, Ph.D. of Authenticity Consulting, LLC, experts in customizing peer coaching groups. In 2004, the Harvard Business Review reported that executive coaching is a $1 billion industry. The industry has only continued to grow. In certain countries, up to 88 percent of companies use coaching, according to What-Is-Coaching's Jean Paul Cortes.

More and more professionals in the last decade have sought out personal coaches to help with addressing complex problems and/or attaining significant goals. Coaches can create a highly personalized approach for each client in an effort to overcome issues and reach those goals. In today's competitive workforce, we can all use a little guidance. There is always room for improvement in our performance, attitude, strategic thinking and organization. A personal coach might be just the thing you need to overcome the obstacles keeping you from your goals.

Along with the value of a personal coach, I took away from that Stanford leadership course a much better understanding of the importance of stage presence. I realized that how you say something can be just as important as what you say. Our message hardly matters if no one is hearing it. Our presentation style may be the biggest reason why our message is not being heard.

After Milo's critique, I got back on that stage and

spoke with conviction. I wanted to be taken seriously. My message mattered, and I wanted my audience to know it. I wanted them to feel what I felt about my job. I wanted them to understand what I was going through. So, I spoke from the heart. I didn't pretty it up or gloss over any details. I was honest and forthright. I looked my classmates in the eyes as I made my way around the stage talking with them. I forged a connection with them during that second speech, something that had been missing the first time around.

I realized it wasn't so much my message that had changed, as much as how I presented it. In my second speech I conveyed my message with confidence, and the result was being heard. I knew that I had something to offer, a strong skill set and the confidence that I could do more. I owned this, and it had made all the difference.

Speaking with Confidence

Most professionals, especially those in management positions, often are required to speak. Part of your job is relaying information effectively. The audience varies, as does the message. You may be required to present your company's annual report to your board of directors one week and talk about your latest product to a group of national users the next. Either way, you need your message to be heard. You need to speak with confidence. When you do, your message will have weight, and those in attendance will be focused and attentive. You may think this is not relevant, but anybody looking to lead in a company has to learn how to sell their idea.

There are a few key things to remember when speaking to a group. If you are struggling with your confidence level, it may behoove you to remember some of these tips. They are nothing new. You probably heard them first from your speech professor in college, but they still apply.

Tip #1: Know your material. This is important, because ultimately confidence has got to come from inside you and whatever mental preparation you have done. No outside entity, trappings, gadgets, slides or paraphernalia can cover for a lack of mental preparation.

Tip #2: Do not hide behind a podium. People connect with people, not with power point presentations. There are many aids you can use when speaking or presenting or arguing a case, but none of them forges the connection you need to build with the audience. The most effective speakers I've seen have nothing between them and the audience. They stand on the edge of the stage and talk to you. A podium is a barrier, blocking you from your audience. Don't decrease your effectiveness behind one.

Tip #3: Be spontaneous. I find it makes my conversations more genuine, refreshing and engaging when there is an element of spontaneity to them. There is no substitute for mental preparation, but be flexible enough to deviate from your script. Every audience is different. Be ready to cater to them. Feel the energy in the room, and be able to play to it. Knowing your material well allows you relax and have fun. When you do, you will bring that audience along with you.

Power Up!

Playing to Your Strengths

Catherine Arnold

Health Care Sector Leader for Equity Research

Credit Suisse

"If they smell blood, they'll pounce." This is what Catherine Arnold was told in her early days as an analyst. In other words, if her colleagues or peers felt she was not confident, there would be a feeding frenzy. If clients felt like she was wavering in confidence or certainty, they would flee.

The last thing Catherine wanted, then, was for anybody to smell blood during meetings with her. She quickly developed strategies to prepare herself thoroughly, so those all-important first impressions were good. Her goal was to get past being unsure if what she knew was appropriate to defend the case.

"You have to walk into the room and, at all costs, focus on what you know, appear confident, but never compromise integrity. If you don't know, say here's what I do know. Leave them with the feeling of confidence that you are in command of your material,"

Catherine explained. She freely admits, however, it took many moments of pain for her to get to that point.

Catherine's career as an analyst came about as a result of her success in the pharmaceutical industry. A graduate of the University of Pittsburgh School of Nursing with an MBA from the Katz Graduate School of Business and MHA from the Graduate School of Public Health at the University of Pittsburgh, Catherine began her career as a Senior Consultant in the Pharmaceutical practice of Booz Allen & Hamilton. From there she joined Hoffman-LaRoche as Director in Strategic Planning/Business Development, reporting directly to the CEO. During her time at Roche, Catherine eventually became the brand director on Xeloda, a breast cancer therapy. Eventually she joined Sanford Bernstein as a Senior Analyst, where she followed European major pharmaceuticals.

Catherine was recruited by Sanford Bernstein because of her vast experience and knowledge in the pharmaceutical industry. It was an alternative path into the financial sector, but one that is not uncommon. Professionals come in from an industry in which they have strong experience and then cover that industry while learning to be an analyst. Although Catherine had never been an analyst before, she learned early on to never say "no" to a new opportunity. So when a colleague linked with a search firm called saying, "We have opportunity for you to join an investment firm as a Wall Street analyst, covering European stocks," she decided to go in and see what the job was about. Catherine remembers the transition to Sanford Bernstein as a very frightening one.

Although she had decided to accept the position, she admits she didn't really understand the role. She initially worked her way from junior to senior analyst. There was no mentoring program at the company, but this was by design. It was a sink-or-swim culture. Basically new hires were given nine months to generate a hypothesis and the supporting research for the role. Catherine credits her penchant for research as a confidence builder during that stressful time. It was little comfort, though, when she saw some people fired weeks before or after their program launch. This is the traditional path for analysts and once they have developed the necessary skills they are promoted.

Her first years as an analyst were focused on survival and pushing her advancement in a very unsupportive environment. There were months of time not meeting with anyone and just sitting in her office doing research while trying to figure out which colleagues' door would be safe to knock on and ask questions. Of the 40 senior staff members, only four were women. And only two of those she felt comfortable enough to confide in. There was also a lot of change. Catherine worked with five bosses in five years. Through all of the challenges of a new career, difficult work environment and uncertainty, Catherine realized she was also developing her confidence. She realized the truth behind the old adage, "What doesn't kill you makes you stronger." She was definitely stronger.

Two things stuck with Catherine as she settled into her role as an analyst, and they continue to guide her: Your motivation can either be the carrot or the stick.

The carrot represents someone pulled with positive reinforcement, while the stick, on the other

hand, represents someone pushed by negative reinforcement.

In all cases, let the carrot be your motivation.
That means you play to your strengths and build up
weak areas. Your first reaction in a new opportunity
may be to panic, thinking about all you don't know. For
example Catherine had never been an analyst. Nagging questions plagued her. How do you know what
you're recommending is right? What if you're not right
about a stock? This was magnified by the fact that
she was working in a very volatile industry with lots
of unexpected events. Your success is based on how
quickly you act and on what you say. "No one wants to
admit they don't know what they don't know - even if
you know what you don't know," Catherine explained.

Catherine had to take a deep breath and remind
herself, "I know the drug industry cold and my com-
petitors who are analysts do not. Play to what they
want to understand." She took that attitude and continued to cultivate stock valuations and the investment piece of the job.

Today, in her role at Credit Suisse, Catherine has

no moments of pain, but it took time to get there, she admits. Two or three years into her new position at Credit Suisse, she began to really feel in command of her domain. Now, she works hard to stay flexible. She firmly believes that being open to new ways of doing things, both personally and professionally, will always keep life interesting.

Have the Confidence to Ask for Help
FORMAL OR INFORMAL MENTORING

Catherine's early entry into her power career was at Sanford Bernstein, where there were no mentoring programs. But at Credit Suisse, mentoring is part of the corporate culture. The company has a formal mentoring program, and staff members are expected to informally mentor colleagues as well. As a result, Catherine now recognizes opportunities for informal mentoring every day. After many meetings, she could sit down with a colleague and say, "Hey, I saw how this played out in the meeting, and here's some advice that will help it go better next time." More often than not, however, Catherine passes up these opportunities. It is not for lack of concern or interest in those around her, but rather a lack of time that prevents her from informally mentoring her younger colleagues.

The scenario playing in Catherine's head as she passes on a chance to mentor someone goes something like this: "If I do this, it'll be an hour-long conversation, and I'll miss out on putting my kids to bed. I am already on the road a lot and miss doing that enough as it is." Does this sound familiar? Though the details may be different, many women regularly deal with struggles like this.

This is why those seeking to be protégés should be not only creative, but also proactive in asking for advice and getting input. Don't wait for someone to approach you. If you feel that a meeting or presentation or project is not progressing the way you would like, go check that feeling out with someone experienced enough to give you direction. This consultation does not have to be face to face. It can be as simple as a brief, concise email with a subject line like: "Quick Question," followed by an explanation (no more than three or four sentences) of your concern and your request for specific feedback. I have found that I am able to provide much more advice and guidance via email than phone conversations or face-to-face meetings. I can control my time better and am not put in the uncomfortable position of having to get someone out of my office, because it is taking too long to get to the point. If you demonstrate a propensity for getting to the point, you are more likely to receive assistance if the need arises in the future. This ability to be concise is especially valuable if you have the opportunity for a face-to-face chat. If you can get in and get out in 15 to 30 minutes, you will likely be remembered for your respect of the mentor's time and your focus and determination.

Using Planning and Metrics to Build Confidence

Knowing that you are doing a good job and adding value to an organization or project is one of the greatest confidence builders available to you in the workplace. As a practice, you should determine what success will look like for any initiative you undertake. Whether your hope is to become a project manager or a new department head, you need to see yourself doing the job and feel what it's like. Maybe you want a new job altogether or you want to start your own business. Either way, the same rule applies. Visualize yourself in that new career, write down your plan of action to get there, find someone you trust and start talking about it. Understand what success in that new position or company looks like for you. Once you've done these things, you are better equipped to move toward that success and to know it once you've attained it. A truly well-defined goal is one that has a much better chance of being achieved.

A frequent joke at Genentech revolved around the reliance on data to make decisions. When seeking to get anything approved by leadership, the motto was "In God we trust. All else must bring the data!" Creating a strategic plan can be key to your progress and increasing success within a company. But that plan is more likely to receive attention if it is supported by data and can identify the results it is likely to bring about. (I detail my first experience with creating a strategic plan in Chapter Six on Lifelong Learning.)

When I was promoted to head the corporate relations group at Genentech, the first task I embarked upon was creating a corporate relations strategic plan for the company. I did not rely solely on my leadership team to create this plan. A big mistake new leaders often make is relying on their own teams or industry trends. This can create a very insular approach to leadership and strategic planning. I took the first two months in my new role to meet with every direct report of the Chief Executive Officer. I also met with every senior vice president, vice president and key functional head in the organization. I only asked for half hour meetings and stuck to that time frame for each meeting. I had only the same three questions for each person with whom I met.

Regarding corporate relations areas of responsibility:

1) What is working?

2) What is not working?

Regarding your functional area in the company:

3) What are the main priorities for your function in the next three to five years?

Not only did this allow me to get up to speed on the key needs and priorities of the company, but it also gave me the opportunity to build new relationships and let leaders know how my department could be of value in helping achieve their goals. It also let leaders know that I valued their opinion and welcomed their input into my area. We were all going to need each other to achieve the tremendous potential provided for us by this company. Collaboration and constant communication were going to be essential to avoiding missteps and maximizing all of the opportunities.

I took notes during each conversation and personally typed them after each session. When I was finished, I had gathered more than 13 pages of typed notes that my leadership team and I pored over with the help of Milo as a facilitator. We found six recurring themes and prioritized them alongside company priorities. This led to a strategic plan which was implemented over a four-year period and was gradually funded as company revenues increased.

In each instance, in order to justify the budget increases, I had to explain what success would look like. In some instances, our C-Suite or other leaders determined the metrics internally. We also used external survey tools more customary to the corporate relations function to validate our work. This included surveying external stakeholders, like physicians, patients, reporters, academics, peers in the biotechnology and pharmaceutical industry, regulatory and public policy influencers as well as patient advocacy and other non-profit entities to get input on performance. We learned the value of identifying and having the means to get feedback from key stakeholders in our industry. Checking in with these groups helped us to get and stay on track.

My confidence in my own abilities and in the abilities of the team I had built increased overwhelmingly during this time. There is no substitute for having a plan or road map to let you and your team know where you're going, how long it may take you and whether or not you have arrived. I used this simple approach to strategic planning at subsequent leadership roles at UnitedHealth Group and Elan Corporation.

Regularly asking simple questions that make you

and other leaders in the company think about what are sometimes very complex issues is the best way to have powerful - strategic and meaningful conversations. Asking them on a regular basis is key here, because we are living and working in a very dynamic environment. We can never assume that what was the best approach last year will still work this year.

Power Up!

MANAGING POWER:

Evelyn DeSalver

Executive VP, Retired

Charles Schwab

During Evelyn DeSalver's very rewarding and exciting career in the financial industry at Charles Schwab, she learned to leverage her influence, sometimes using her authority, sometimes giving control away. "I give my power away a lot, but when I do, it is deliberate. I do it so other people feel empowered to make good decisions. In my opinion, this is simply sharing what I have, so other people can shine," she explained.

Of course, there have been times when Evelyn has needed to maintain her control. "At a board meeting, one member was worried whether I could handle an individual who was more of a bully on the board," she explained. "I told the concerned board member that I wasn't worried, because all of us were in a partnership. The other member can act like a bully, but at end of day we have to reach a good business conclusion. And we did." So one of the ways Evelyn maintains her authority is by remaining focused on the end goal. "I actually see this as sharing power in a sense, because if everyone knows what you are trying to achieve and the focus is on business issues rather than personal issues, everyone will be successful," she said.

There are a lot of ways that we need to think about and approach using the influence we have. When Evelyn was promoted into her final role at Schwab, the person she replaced was promoted into a new role. The two were peers and respected each other a lot. Evelyn got the job of her predecessor, but not his title of Executive Vice President. The human resources department had decided to maintain her "Senior Vice President" title, though the move was a promotion. When her boss's boss called to congratulate her, Evelyn said "Thanks, but I'm really disappointed that it's not an Executive Vice President position. I think this needs to be an Executive Vice President position." He agreed with her and pushed it through. "In that instance I used the power of a strong relationship to say 'I deserve this' and achieved a significant milestone in my career," she said.

Evelyn cautions that she used her influence judiciously. If she had come to work every day whining about not getting a position she deserved, she wouldn't have been thought worthy of the new role. Instead, she spoke up at just the right time and was not afraid to ask questions. In the case of her promotion, she had assumed, since human resources left her at the senior vice president title in her new role, that they were told to do so. It turned out that the human resources staff knew the company was downsizing and was only seeking to reduce the number of officers.

Assuming that only those in leadership positions have power is another mistake Evelyn cautions against. At one point in her career, Evelyn was the chief of staff to the president of the company. The president had 12 direct reports and was focused on getting things off of his plate, so he could focus more on strategic planning. In her support role of chief of staff, she held a lof of indirect power. But this power was exercised through influence rather than direct authority.

In Evelyn's opinion, the worst kind of person in this role is the one who tries to use her office to get recognition or further her own agenda. Indirectly a position like this carries a lot of power, but it's important for someone in this role to remember to use caution when exercising it. She calls a role like this one the "wonder bra position," an invisible means of support. If you are doing a great job the boss will never know it. You can't say to him or her, "I just saved your butt."

Throughout her career, Evelyn has made a point of helping other women and young girls understand the strength they have. Several years ago, she became involved with a non-profit organization called the Women's Initiative for Self-Employment. When she was recommended as a potential board member, she met with the Executive Director and was very impressed. In addition to being on the board, Evelyn ran a volleyball program for sixth to eighth-grade girls. She feels sports help girls become conscious of who they are and the power they have individually as well as collectively as a team. Her main point being that it is never too early to start girls on the path to self-confidence and there are many venues to aid this development including organized sports and access to accomplished female role models.

The Women's Initiative's overall mission is to help lower-income women become economically independent by giving them training and resources. Evelyn believes this helps them realize that they have personal power and can overcome the financial mindset that men earn the money and women don't. Allowing them to become economically independent by starting their own business also helps them overcome the fear of success and fear of having money, because they have to figure out how to make right choices with the money they will have available to them through their new business.

Many of the women who join the Women's Initiative are single moms coming out of abusive relationships. In the program, women receive mentoring and counseling. Once a woman graduates from the program, she can apply for a loan to start her own business. Most do not have a credit history, so they cannot go to traditional banks for a loan. Thirty-five percent of the graduates double their income within the first year. Evelyn sees this process spawn a positive cycle that changes the lives of many women and moves them toward independence and self-sufficiency. As the women become more empowered, they often volunteer and contribute back to the community, sometimes even hiring other women in the community.

Evelyn is now the Chairman of the Board for the Women's Initiative. The organization's founder and board chair quit right after Evelyn joined, so she had to totally resurrect the board and the 20-year-old organization. "When I started to realize the impact on communities and the opportunity to help women get out of poverty while also realizing their potential, it was an easy commitment to make." Evelyn continues to give away, or share, her power. For now, it's Evelyn challenging these underprivileged women, but she hopes that it will one day be them passing on what they've learned from her. (More on the Women's Health Initiative is discussed in Chapter 4.)

Ask Mary

I feel like my boss and colleagues ignore me. How can I get the attention I desire?

This question came from a young protégé of mine who works in the human resources department of a large hospital. She was very frustrated by her role in a large department, because she felt she was not being taken seriously by her boss and colleagues. In staff meetings she would frequently offer ideas or suggestions that were not even acknowledged, while others might later offer the same ideas and get credit. She did not feel included and a part of the team.

My own observation was that this lovely woman

just did not resonate a strong presence. She easily blended into the crowd. She did not have a strong voice, and I could see how she could be overlooked. My advice was that, instead of just waiting on someone to acknowledge her in a staff meeting, she go meet one-on-one with various colleagues, including her boss. The point was to let them get to know her and her skills and ideas, so that they would not only be hearing from her in the department meetings, where everyone was jockeying for attention.

I also advised her to volunteer to work on a major initiative or even a project that others might shun. By doing this, she would gain the opportunity to demonstrate her abilities, rather than just trying to talk to people about them. In her case, actions would speak louder than her words.

Another tip for being heard in a room full of ideas is to get up and go to the board and write or illustrate your idea instead of just trying to out-talk everyone else. In these instances, it is wise to be concise, clear with your ideas and have outcomes well thought out. You can also volunteer to form a subcommittee of the

department to address a particular problem or individually take on one or more follow-up action steps that
will allow you the opportunity to speak and be heard
in subsequent meetings.

Finally, I advised my protégé to find opportunities to practice speaking and projecting her voice.
Taking a theater class at a community college can provide this training. So can joining a speaker's group like
Toastmasters.

Confidence Building Highlights

- According to Dr. James Milojkovich, the most important thing we can do in life is show up. This means
being fully present in the moment as our true powerful selves by being aware and in control of how
we come across to others, listening to others with
an open mind and articulating based on our heart or
convictions – not just our heads.

- When we understand who we are, what we value and
what we can contribute to our family or our company, we gain confidence.

- When we are confident, people will pay attention.

They will listen to us and believe us.

- Confidence is key to your success, both professionally and personally.

- Knowing you are doing a good job and adding value to an organization or project is one of the greatest confidence builders available to you in the workplace.

- Always be in command of your material. Walk into the room and focus on what you know. But, remember to never compromise integrity. If you don't know, say "Here's what I do know."

- Stage presence and presentation matter. You are the message. Put no barriers between yourself and your audience. Speak with conviction, and you will be heard.

- As a practice, you should determine what success will look like for any initiative you undertake. Then, you will know when you have arrived.

- A personal coach is an asset. Get one if you can. Having a trusted third party to bounce ideas off of as you're managing your staff and workload can be invaluable so that you maintain a balance of strategic focus.

- Use your power judiciously. Let it work for you when there is cause and share it when you can.

Chapter Two
Work and Life – Finding Your Balance!
"Alone we find happiness. Together we find love"
- Unknown

I was in graduate school at USC and working full time at Kaiser. I had prepared my family for this. My company was supportive, and I was enjoying (and doing well in) all of the courses. But I hit a wall.

I strongly believe in including my family in my decision-making process. So, when I made the decision, based on the recommendation of both my mentor and boss, to enroll in graduate school and pursue a Master of Health Administration degree, I had a conversation with my kids. I explained to them why Mommy would be in class on weekends and not able to go to games and church on Sundays for a while. I explained to them about work and salaries and promotions and how going to graduate school would allow me to be promoted and help assure a better future for our whole family. I told them that, even though I was a regional manager now, going to graduate school would one day enable me to be promoted to vice president at a company. They understood, and after I had completed my degree, frequently asked me if I'd made vice president yet! (More on this in chapter five.) But, being in graduate school and working full time with three children can be challenging, to say the least. It wasn't long before I was ready to quit school. I was totally overwhelmed. I needed to talk to someone who could see my situation from a different perspective, so I made a call.

Counselor: "Hello?"

Me: "Yes, hello sir. I understand this is a free counseling service that my employer provides?"

Counselor: "Yes it is."

Me: "Great. Well I just want to talk to someone because I'm in graduate school, working full time with a husband and three children – and my whole family has gone crazy. Well, either it's them or it's me. I'm not sure which. But just tell me if it's me, because I think I need to quit graduate school. You see my husband and kids are..."

Counselor: "Well, first of all, why don't you tell me about you"

Me: "Umm, okay."

Counselor: "How are you doing in graduate school?"

Me: "Oh, I'm actually doing great. I love it. I haven't felt this stimulated and challenged in years. I'm getting great grades. I love my school, and my classmates are so supportive, but I don't know what's wrong with my...."

Counselor: "What are you majoring in?"

Me: "I'm getting a Masters Degree in Health Administration."

Counselor: "What are you going to do when you're done?"

Me: "I want to advance at my job and take on a role with greater responsibility. I've been thinking about trying my hand at business consulting."

Counselor: "How much longer before you're done?"

Me: "Well, it's a three-year program, but I've

been doubling my classes, and my company will let me do a combined residency with my job, so I'll be done in two years, which is really great. I have about six months left."

Counselor: "Well, congratulations. It sounds like you're doing great. You're focused, on target, and you're almost done."

Me: "Well, yes, I guess that's true. Wow! I hadn't really thought about it that way. Geez, well, I guess graduate school won't be an issue pretty soon, huh?

Counselor: "No. You're almost there. Just stay focused."

Me: "I will. And thank you so much for listening."

Counselor: "You're welcome."

In my mind, graduate school had been causing discord in my family. But by getting me to talk about why I enrolled in school and how much I felt energized and stimulated by being back in an academic environment, the counselor helped me to feel differently and resurrect my original motivation. Suddenly, I was able to patiently deal with my family, while still enjoying the pursuit of my goals. Once I could think rationally again, I realized I could solve some of the issues by simply taking a couple of days of vacation and making some schedule adjustments.

There is a significant amount of personal sacrifice involved in any major accomplishment. We women strive to have it all, but there is always a cost. It has been said again and again, that we can have it all, but not at the same time. I would agree, but we can find a balance when we prioritize our choices.

When I was in graduate school, I lost out on time with my family. If I had chosen to quit school, I would have missed out on promotions and other opportunities at work. There was no easy choice, there was always guilt, and there was always sacrifice. But I realized I could make it through by looking at the things I valued, making choices based on those values, and creating a list of priorities.

Choice + Prioritization = Balance

You have made choices in your life that have gotten you to where you are now. I made the choice to get married, have children and have a career. Whether your choices were similar to mine or, instead, you chose a different path, maybe to focus on your career and remain single, there is a need to look at your life choices when challenges arise.

When you find yourself at a crossroads or with your life feeling off kilter, either personally or professionally, it is important to figure out what matters most to you. According to personal coach Laura Berman Fortgang, author of NOW WHAT? 90 Days to a New Life Direction, getting your priorities clear is the first and most essential step toward achieving a well-balanced life. She suggests writing down a list of your top 5 priorities. The key to this exercise is to be honest with yourself, and instead of listing what you think your priorities should be, list what you want them to be.

Create a List of Priorities

After listing your priorities, analyze where you are spending the bulk of your time. Is your time being spent on your priorities? If not, it may be time to drop some of the activities that didn't make it onto your priorities list. Dropping these unnecessary activities will help you restructure your time, giving more of it to the things you most value. It may be hard to let go of certain projects or commitments at first, but once you do, you will feel more centered and focused. Letting things go brings with it a measure of peace.

Our priorities list may include things like family, career, spirituality, community service, education and health. Too often, however, we forget to make ourselves a part of that list. Remember, you are a priority and need nurturing. Carve out time for yourself. Meditate or do 20 minutes of stretching in the morning. Also find time at least five days a week to do cardiovascular exercise like walking, jogging or aerobics. As we get older, it is also important to lift weights to maintain muscle strength. Plan a spa day every six months or long weekends every quarter, so you can refocus, de-stress and enjoy yourself.

It turns out, vacations may be key to your continued success at home and at work. Evidence from researchers at the Marshfield Clinic in Wisconsin reveals that women who take frequent vacations are less likely to become stressed out or depressed. In addition, women who take time to get away report a higher rate of marital satisfaction. The study, published in a November, 2005 issue of the Wisconsin Medical Journal, was conducted from 1996 through 2001 and involved a random sample of 1,500 women from central Wisconsin. The researchers set out to look at stress, quality of marital life, and disruptive life at home due to work in women who vacationed frequently versus those who did not. "I think women have less on their minds and do not have the need to constantly multi-task when they take vacations," explained Catherine A. McCarty, Ph.D., M.P.H., a senior epidemiologist and director of the Center for Human Genetics at the Marshfield Clinic Research Foundation.

These little treats you set out through the year will keep you mentally and physically replenished and increase your productivity in all areas of your life. What might feel a little selfish at the beginning is, in actuality, the most selfless of actions. When you take care of yourself, you can better take care of others.

Your family and your company will benefit from your "me" time.

Finding Your Balance

This chapter is such a hot button for all of the women interviewed for this book. Most of them felt compelled to comment on it, even when it wasn't the primary focus of their story. This is also one of the most popular topics during my speaking engagements. As a result, I have talked with many people over the years about their challenges.

What I am hearing is, without a doubt, the biggest struggle for working women who want to advance and keep making progress is striking a balance between work and family. For many of us, family and career sit at the top of our priorities list. Many women cannot progress in successful careers, however, until they have thought through and resolved how to handle the delicate balance these two areas require. The bottom line is that there will never be one simple solution that can be employed at all times. Yes, even this will shift and change throughout your career. In fact what human resources professionals used to call work/life balance they now call work/life choices.

Years ago, when I first started hearing complaints and concerns from women (and a few younger men with wives unhappy about their time away from home) about work life balance, they wanted to know what the company was going to do about workloads or work hours or staffing to help address work/life balance. Some people even got angry and left companies because they felt it was the company's fault or boss' fault that they did not have any work/life balance. No matter how generous your employer may be and how many services are provided, your employer or your immediate supervisor will never balance your work or control your personal life. These are your choices, and only you and your family are responsible for making these decisions.

In an ideal world, couples begin planning how to manage these shifts before they have the first child. Please note the emphasis on couples here, because the first strategy for dealing with work/life conflicts is to remind married women that these are family issues and choices – not just personal ones. Reaching agreement on when to have children, how every family member will help and what kind of support network will be needed is crucial. There is no cookie cutter approach. I have worked with and mentored women who decided to delay having children, women who proceeded to have children while both parents worked, women whose spouses stayed home to care for children, single moms and women who quit work to care for their children. The main point is that choices have to be made, and you have to be realistic and honest when you are making them. You and your spouse should be on the same page with whatever you choose. If you are not, resentment may build, and down the road, you may experience trouble in the relationship because of the choices you made early on. The point is that, as a couple, the choices you make should not just make you comfortable. They should be choices you can both be excited about.

In the early years of my career, when I was also having children, we didn't have any choice. For economic reasons, both my husband and I had to work.

While we did not live close to either of our families, we already had a strong network of friends in our church with multiple family home daycare options. We also had friends who could be called in emergencies to pick up our kids before or after school, get them to practices and so forth. We were very fortunate that the stay-at-home moms or moms who worked close by were more than willing to help the working and commuting moms. Planning in advance and asking for help is mandatory and should not invoke guilt.

Of course, there is no plan that can account for a 12-year old son who tells you at 7 a.m. that, by the way, he forgot to tell you last night that he told his class he would provide something for today's potluck lunch. "Oh, fine," you're thinking as you figure you can make a quick stop by the grocery store to grab a salad or chips or drinks – simple, quick stuff your daughters instinctively know to sign you up for.-- only to be stopped in your tracks when you find out he's signed you up for friend chicken and cornbread. And, of course, it's on a day you have coordinated a major meeting for the CEO and other senior executives, as well as out of town guests. It is a meeting you absolutely cannot miss.

"Well is anybody else bringing a main dish?" I asked my son.

"No, I told everybody you would make enough for the entire class," he said, full of innocence.

When I saw the anguish on his face, I stifled my own frustration and said, "Okay, I'll figure something out."

This is where having an understanding assistant, co-worker or family friend is incredibly helpful. Once in the office, I shared my dilemma with my assistant, Pearl, (along with other assorted staff members), and once they managed to pull themselves together long enough to stop laughing, I asked for help. Pearl promised to figure something out by lunchtime. Since there was no take out in San Francisco that delivered fried chicken and cornbread, Pearl ended up paying a visit to the Colonel and making a food drop for me with a note to the teacher apologizing that I couldn't personally prepare my son's favorite dishes (the ones he'd bragged to his classmates about) but promising that I would definitely prepare them next time. Even though many of us have moved on to other companies, whenever we see each other, we still laugh about "Baby Brother" (my son's nickname given to him at birth by his middle sister) signing me up to make fried chicken and corn bread for his middle school class.

I couldn't have gotten through that event or that day successfully without help. I made sure to thank Pearl and those who came to my aid. More powerful than my thanks, however, is the knowledge that they know I would help them, too. If there is another mom, friend or family member who comes to your aid, you'll need to be prepared to return the favor if the opportunity presents itself. Reciprocity is the most powerful choice you have when relying on family and friends for help. They will always remain willing to help you, if they know you are not only grateful, but willing to help them in return.

After I was promoted to run my department at Genentech, my schedule and commitments escalated almost exponentially. My department grew from 16 people and an approximately $14 million budget per year to 43 people and $100 million in a four-year period. I had to become very creative in getting the needs of my family met. A big challenge was getting home early enough to cook dinner. Meetings frequently ran late, and traffic was very unpredictable. I tried picking up some of the meals from the cafeteria at work, but my picky eaters at home frequently did not care for them. Often times, we ended up eating out late at night.

During this time, a close friend from church was laid off, and she approached me and a few other executive women about an idea she had for a business. She loved to cook and noticed, as I did, the various food companies that prepared and delivered home-cooked meals were not servicing our area. She proposed preparing healthy meals for us. I knew my family liked her cooking, so she had an instant customer. This proved to be such a relief. She lived close by, and she delivered the meals to my home if I wasn't available to pick them up. I didn't have to worry about my kids eating healthy. We didn't have to spend late nights out eating, despite my schedule. I can't emphasize enough the help this provided me, and it was helpful to her too. She received the interim financial support she needed, and I received the piece of mind of knowing my family had good, healthy meals. Do not hesitate to ask for or offer help. There are a lot of solutions out there if you just explore a little.

It is important to remember those who care about you want you to succeed. They are often looking for ways to help, so they can contribute to your success. You may be surprised at the willingness of your family and friends to come to your aid. You just need the courage to ask.

Ask Mary

Can you provide some advice on how a professional woman carries herself without giving people the wrong perception about her? I am responsible for training diverse groups of people at my company. Some of them may have never had a woman telling them how to do their job, and I'm running into some perception problems. I'm sure many of the perception problems are cultural, but I need to change something about myself "professionally," and

I'm just not sure what it is or how to change it.

I had several enjoyable conversations with this protégé and wanted to share her enlightening story with you. While my response to this Ask Mary question may be a little longer than the others, the question itself crosses several key areas being discussed in this book, including confidence building and work/life choices. It paints such a complete picture of the complexity of the dilemmas women face who are seeking to progress to more powerful positions while balancing priorities.

My questioner trains new employees for her company. It's a job she has been in for about two years. She does not have a college degree and is self-taught in her newly created role, because the company had no training program for her. She worked her way up in the company and was really good at what she did, so the company promoted her to a trainer role. It is a new position for her and for the company.

She initially covered the northern region of her state. In the past year, however, she was given responsibility for training the new employees in the entire state. This increased responsibility also meant she had to travel statewide.

So, she has no predecessor, role model or mentor to show her the way. Her boss is not an expert and has no background in training either. Recent feedback given to her manager by current class participants is that she is too harsh. She wants to know how she can change this perception. In her mind, she feels she is training adults and should not have to speak to them like kids. She is not sure if the feedback relates to cultural differences, since it is a very diverse class. She thinks the class is focusing on her, instead of on learning.

Before giving her any feedback, I probed a little deeper:

"What are you thinking when you show up at work every day?" I asked.

"When I wake up in the morning, I ask myself, am I smart enough to do this?" she said. "Will I be able to remember the material? Will I be able to function in front of these people? I have to mentally prepare myself to face the people, and therefore, I just come in and get right to the subject matter."

She went on to confide that she doesn't like traveling so much and worries about leaving her husband at home alone so much. With her expanded duties, she is away doing trainings for up to two months at a time.

I shared with her that people who are perceived as being too harsh or too hard- nosed are coming across as compassionless. I went on to share that years earlier, when I received feedback about not showing compassion, it was because I was overwhelmed with trying to juggle a huge issue at work and personal issues at home. My behavior at work was reflecting my concerns about home, even if I never stated those concerns.

This is the area where a lot of women trip up, because we don't see it happening. We try to separate the work issues from personal issues. We come to work and try to perform our duties as though the personal ones do not matter. But, often it is your personal issues that are impacting your work performance.

"You are going to have to make some choices," I

explained to the job trainer. You are going to have to communicate more with your boss and your husband, and you are going to have to set some boundaries with both. Let your boss know that you need some help in this role. Let your husband know the pressure you are feeling and that you need his support and honest communication. Sharing this may actually help build more intimacy between you and your spouse as you lower your "super woman" façade with him.

Fortunately, when her boss gave her initial feedback, she listened and did not get defensive, even though she was not pleased about the comments. I advised her to go back to her boss as a follow up to the feedback conversation. I advised her to let him know that all of the travel was putting a strain on her family and until more help was hired, she needed to space out the trainings more, so that she was not on the road for more than a month or two at a time. I told her to frame the conversation and request as planning, rather than complaining, as she and her boss working together to come up with a solution. It was best to go into that meeting positively, rather than as being mad at the world. She just needed to acknowledge that it had been a little more tense at work than usual. Her husband had been complaining, because she was gone so much.

Then we focused on the conversation with her husband. She explained that she used to come home on weekends, but it had become too much of a hassle. She was rushing to and from the airport and seemed only to be home long enough to do laundry before it was time to leave. She also admitted one of the main reasons she wants to come home is to be able to go to church on Sundays. Her husband would prefer her to spend that time with him, however, since he has to go to work on Sunday afternoons.

At one point they were alternating weekends. He would come see her every other weekend, so she did not have to travel as often, but that got too expensive. However, the company pays for her trips home. I paused for a moment. "Well then Sweetie," I said in my nicest voice. "You need to come home on weekends."

A flight to the southern part of the state is only

one hour, I reminded her. Stay over, and take the Monday morning flight, so then you can have three evenings at home. "Wow, that means I have to get up really early on Monday," she said.

"Yes, that means you have to catch a 6 a.m. flight to get to the office by 8 a.m., but it's not like you have anything to do in the evenings, so you can get to bed early," I explained.

I also advised her to find a church near her corporate apartment and go to Wednesday evening services. The bottom line is that she liked her job and wanted to advance in her career. She was going to have to make some sacrifices or get a new job. Getting a new husband wouldn't solve the problem I joked, because a new one might want to spend more time with you.

What about the perceptions?

So, we worked out some ways she could improve her home life. She and her husband, with a little effort, could have more time together. By working on this aspect of her life, certain problems she was having in her training classes would go away, I assured her. Her lack of guilt and stress regarding her home life would show in her ability to relax at work. Her classes would sense her ease and follow her lead.

Rather than coming into class with a drill sergeant mentality, spouting off rules, regulations and expectations of the company right off the bat, I advised her to find some ways to connect with her students first, lightening up the mood and setting a tone for the duration of the class. Introductions are always a good place to start. Ice-breaker exercises also allow students to relax and get to know one another. Human resources staff usually have great resources for these types of exercises.

Allow more time for interaction in the class. Let classmates take a shot at answering questions, so everybody is not focusing on you as the trainer.

I reminded her that she knows the material thoroughly, whereas they are just learning it, and therefore, they can probably understand the questions better than she can. It is new and fresh in their minds, ready to be turned over and analyzed.

"Remember," I said "they are there to thoroughly understand the material, so they can become productive members of the company. Their success is a reflection on you as well."

She laughed and admitted that sometimes she can be a drill sergeant. Class feedback also indicated that sometimes the students were afraid to ask questions. She also confided that one student did try to help answer questions for students who were struggling, and she felt the student was trying to imply that she didn't know her material. She actually moved the woman's seat in class, so that she no longer sat next to one particular woman who was having difficulties!

My advice was to let the students take part, to help each other and her. Everyone would benefit from an inclusive approach. I got her to understand having an engaging class, with students eager to participate was a blessing, not a poor reflection on her teaching skills. Only students paying attention ask questions. Only students whose interests have been sparked can answer them. She should want both.

Power Up!

Powerful Career Women Speak on Priorities and Work/Life Choices

While most chapters will feature one or two Power Up! profiles, almost all of the women profiled had very strong opinions about work/life choices so I have included all of those comments in this section.

Catherine Arnold

Senior Healthcare Analyst

Credit Suisse

"Your premise that women do not provide more mentoring due to their roles as primary caregivers is good," Catherine told me, when we talked about how she grew into her career. She, like many of the other women I talked to for this book, was loath to leave the discussion before opening up about finding, or at least working toward, her own work/life balance.

Catherine considers herself very fortunate that her husband is more helpful than the average husband who works full time. He is a lawyer and helps out with fifty percent of the housework, if not more. Catherine works more hours than he does. So, it only seems fair. "Nevertheless," she said, "there are places he will never go." There are certain things that will always be "Catherine's to do" – things like buying birthday presents, picking out Christmas cards or figuring out what Halloween costumes the children will wear.

Catherine believes women have rolling to-do lists in their heads. The slew of personal things that need to get done simultaneously, that juggling that goes on internally as well as externally in women's lives, guess what? Many men don't know or care about most of those things. They don't have a checklist, and for the most part, don't care if those things get done. It is a fundamental difference in our approaches to work and home life. Many women must split their focus. And for some powerful women, like Catherine, that split impacts her ability to be a formal mentor or even provide as much informal mentoring during this time when her children are young.

Evelyn DeSalver
EVP, Retired

Charles Schwab

When asked about work/life balance, Evelyn DeSalver recalled making the hard choice to commute cross-country to work. Although Evelyn lived in Northern California, she accepted a promotion at Charles Schwab's New York office. This decision required her to commute back and forth from New York to San Francisco for three years. She came home every other weekend during this time.

Evelyn knew that making this career decision was risky. It demanded a lot of her, physically and mentally to maintain a long-term, long-distance situation with her family. She chose to do it, because she knew she was ready for the next phase of her career to begin. She had not anticipated getting there would require her to commute, but Evelyn understood that taking advantage of opportunities often demands taking risks. What those risks will be, Evelyn explained, are not always clear when you begin charting the course for your career. "People want such a firm path to the next level, but the truth is you never know how firm any path is. It's not always a straight path," Evelyn said looking back.

More important than knowing you are willing to take a risk is knowing your risk threshold, Evelyn stressed. The promotion in New York turned out to be lucrative for Evelyn from a career standpoint, but there was more to consider. The physical toll the commuting began to take on Evelyn could not be ignored. The risk to her body was not something Evelyn had considered upon accepting the position, but it began to show itself over time. "Sometimes our head tells us something different than our bodies. We tend to keep listening to our head, which tells us we can do it. Our body may be saying 'stop,' but we have a tendency to ignore it," Evelyn said.

During this time in her career Evelyn took care of every body in her family except her own. She did not go to the gym, she didn't take long walks or relax through meditation. The one hour she reserved for herself every day was the time she used going to the grocery store or running other errands. "Women cater to their spouses, work, kids, but don't take care of themselves. Mainly, this happens, because women feel guilty," Evelyn said. "Guilt can be very debilitating for many women."

Women can be both ambitious and still have that work/life balance, but we too often do it at a cost to ourselves, Evelyn said. If we approach everything with an understanding of the risks involved, both physically and mentally, we might ask for help. Doing this would preserve us physically, reduce our guilt of not being everywhere at once and create some internal harmony.

We can't, and many times don't want to, avoid risk. Taking risks allow us to grow. We just need to remember to ask ourselves, "Where is my risk threshold?" At what point does the cost outweigh the benefit? When you answer that question, you will be better able to take the chances that will reap benefits in the end.

Kim Thiboldeaux
President and CEO The Cancer Support Community
(Formerly The Wellness Community and Gilda's Club
Worldwide)

Author, The Total Cancer Wellness Guide

Kim has taken different approach to work/life choices. She made the decision not to get married or have kids. She grew up in a close, tight-knit family with a stay-at-home mom. She always felt that if she was going to have a family, she would want to be home for them, too. She knew she would want to raise her children herself, without day care or nannies doing the bulk of the work. It was what her mother had done, and it was what she expected she would do as well.

After much introspection, Kim decided getting married and having children were not things she felt called to do. Her focus and energy were naturally chan-neled in a different direction, and as time went on, she recognized and accepted that. Kim realized she felt obligated to use the skills and talents she has been given to advance the cause and mission of The Can-cer Support Center. She felt called to use her energy, skills and talents to do good, meaningful and transfor-mational things in her life and in the lives of others.

That is not to say Kim lacks family in her life. To the contrary, she has eight nieces and nephews and dotes on them. She is able to invest a lot of quality time with each of them and treasures those opportunities. She says she has been able to figure out how to have family and kids in her life in a different way, one that works better with her active lifestyle.

Traveling plays a key role in Kim's lifestyle. So, while she works long hours in an intense job, she finds balance through her travels. She is passionate about experiencing other cultures and seeing first-hand how to live life in new and different ways. It invigorates Kim to walk through ancient cities and dine on exotic cuisine. She is not much for wiling away the day on the sand at the beach, but give her ruins to explore or a trail to hike, and she is game for the experience, energized by the possibility of discovery.

Rather than wear her out, this type of traveling, physically challenging though it may be, helps to rest and revive Kim. It creates a real departure from everyday life, and her rested brain often surprises her when she returns from these sojourns. She comes back to work with new ideas and new ways to approach things, even though she wasn't thinking about work while on vacation.

"You've got to step away. Recognize it will only make you better leader, co-worker or boss," she advises. "People are astonished that I am a CEO, and yet I will go abroad for two or three weeks. That's part of the balance I have created in my life. That nurtures and sustains me, while for other women that sustenance may come from being a mother and having kids." Kim does not travel alone. "I do take my nieces and nephews on trips with me, and they frequently stay over with me. I think it gives each of them something special and unique that they don't necessarily get in [their] parental relationships," she said.

While Kim's path and lifestyle are, of course, her own, she encourages other women to feel like they can explore all of their options in life. "You do have the choice, and there are other ways to have family. It is liberating and exciting and enlightening for women to know that there are other choices," she said.

Dr. Marianne Legato, M.D., F.A.C.P.
Author, Why Men Never Remember and Women Never

Forget

Founder, Partnership for Gender-Specific Medicine at Columbia University College of Physicians and Surgeons

Whether we want to admit it or not, whether we agree or not, statistically speaking women tend to handle the majority of child-rearing responsibilities in most households. Most of these women will admit that even on their best days, parenting is a difficult job. Dr. Marianne Legato recalls seeing her own father once a year growing up. When he did have vacation time and could have visited his children, he chose to go hunting by himself instead.

The burden for raising children naturally falls to the mother. Even in those situations where the father is present, it is most often the mother who schedules piano lessons, makes sure homework is done and gets lunchboxes ready. Most of us feel this is our job as mothers, and that is okay. What isn't okay, according to Marianne, is beating ourselves up for not being perfect at it. We have to understand that we are not perfect at anything, and we never will be. We can be pretty good at it, sometimes great, but never perfect.

Understanding that and then accepting it can go a long way toward maintaining our sanity and preserving our happiness.

There are ages at which children are needy, and, despite what you have going on at work, you have to put them first. That does not mean you can't return later to the work, and spend a little time at night catching up a little bit. "We all have to accept the fact that the demands of the day are demands of the day, and not every day will you be able to be everywhere at every time," explained Marianne. "If you write a list of what will happen to you tomorrow from breakfast until the end of the day, you can't even tell me what will happen at breakfast. The pace of life is that fast and that dynamic - ever changing."

Marianne suggests looking at the moment. Find your successes in them, and know that there are many more on their way. We will have great successes and, sometimes, great failures all in the course of a day. That's the way it is. We are not perfect. We can't do it all. But, we can relax, and do the best we can at the moment.

Dr. Beverly Tatum, Ph.D
President
Spelman College

Becoming President of Spelman College in 2002 was not an easy decision for Dr. Beverly Daniel Tatum. Although it was a wonderful opportunity, it presented a major work/life choice challenge. "My family lives in Massachusetts, so accepting the job meant relocation to Atlanta," she explained. "My son was a sophomore in high school and about to go into his junior year. My husband and I did not want to disrupt his high school experience. He had lived in the same home since he was born, and we did not feel it was in his best interest to move. Also, my husband had been in his job a long time and was soon going to be eligible for early retirement. The conversation we had to have was should I even consider the opportunity."

Dr. Tatum and her family recognized it was a unique opportunity. There is only one Spelman, they reasoned. Dr. Tatum, if chosen to serve as president, would be only the ninth president of Spelman and have a chance to impact many young lives at the private, liberal arts, historically black college for women. "If I pursued it and did not get it, that was great. But if I pursued it and was successful, it meant a long-term commitment, because whoever became president would be in the role for some time. Both my husband and son said, 'If you don't pursue this, you will always regret it,'" Dr. Tatum remembered. She knew they were right.

Together the family made the decision for Dr. Tatum to pursue the opportunity. They agreed, also, that if she were elected, she would accept the position and go to Atlanta alone. "My husband and son would stay in Massachusetts for two years and then follow me to Atlanta," she explained. "I had never been in a commuter relationship before and did not want to mess up a good thing. I also felt strongly that it was better for my son to stay where he was rather than start all over again as a junior at a new high school in a totally different part of the country. So, for a long time, I commuted home on weekends as often as possible, and my husband and son also periodically came to Atlanta for the weekend."

While the choice to pursue a once-in-a-lifetime career opportunity that might prove disruptive to her family was a difficult one for Dr. Tatum, she believes it has brought about unexpected rewards. "It is possible for things to work out for everybody. Our situation actually proved to be an important bonding opportunity for my son and his father," she said.

Mara Aspinall
President & CEO, On-Q-ity

Mara likes the idea of "mini-mentoring" because she feels we need different mentors for different situations in life or at work. She frequently provides what she calls mini-mentoring to women about her approach to balancing work and personal life.

Mara and her husband have two sons both born during the time she worked at Bain Consulting. She went back to work 10 days after each of her sons were born. She had no job pressure to go back to work, but she chose to do it. Despite that, it was the toughest time for her, personally, because of how female colleagues reacted to her choice to return to work so soon after childbirth. There were very few senior women and those women, as well as women aspiring to senior roles, became angry with her, no longer looking to her as a mentor because they worried that if the company saw this as an acceptable standard they would be pressured to come back in 10 days as well. But Mara remained resolute. She had made this choice for herself. She was not going to stay home because of expectation.

The wife of another Bain partner, Jeff, who sat two doors down from Mara's office, had a baby on the same day, just two hours apart from Mara. Jeff and Mara returned to work on the same day – 10 days after the birth of each of their children. On the day she returned, a female senior partner came to her office and asked her, "Is the baby okay? Did the baby die?" When Mara said "no," the senior partner responded, "then why are you here?" Mara looked at her and said, "Jeff is back. Did you ask Jeff who is taking care of his baby or ask him why he is back so quickly or who is taking care of the baby?" In retrospect, Mara realizes the senior partner's questions were well-intentioned, but the woman knew no other explanation. Mara still gets emotional about this treatment even now, 18 years later. Mara explains her rationale for going back to work so soon. In her mind, the baby was not going through any major milestones. She didn't need to be there 24 hours a day to do things that were being done very well by her nanny.

Fifteen months later, after the birth of her second son, she went back to work – again in 10 days. She worked a flexible schedule, working four days a week, in order to spend time with her older child. However, Mara does note that once her kids were in junior high and high school that they began to let her know they wanted more of her time saying, "Mom, a lot of other parents show up more than you do." She then made adjustments in her schedule so that she could participate in more academic and extracurricular activities with them. Mara takes pride in knowing everything about her kids, and when they need her, she can and will be there, taking advantage of being an executive with flexibility.

It is important to Mara that she separates work

and home. Interestingly, one of the ways she does that is to never put pictures in her office. In other words, she keeps work at work and home is for family. Although she has received lots of antagonism, Mara notes that she had "closet" protégés, other women who felt the same way. Even today, women who don't want to stay home with the baby find their way to her, and she tells them its okay to not want to be home. However, perceptions haven't changed much in 18 years. She says most women still look at her funny when she talks about it.

Eunice Azzani

CEO, Azzani Search

Former Principal Partner, Korn-Ferry Executive Recruiting

Eunice, like so many of the women profiled in this book and the many women I have met speaking and traveling, understands that work and life are all about choices. There will never be true balance, but rather a focus on different priorities at different seasons of your life. She feels it's necessary to stress this point, as she did with me, when talking with other women, too. We cannot be all things to all people at the same time. We have to learn how to juggle, and women make very good jugglers.

Men can focus on just one thing, Eunice explained. Unfortunately, our culture feels fine about that. The same is not the case for women, however. We are expected to take on responsibility for many things at once. Our strength, then, comes from our ability to multi-task, learning to deal with a wide spectrum of things from home life to work life, and it can work to our benefit if we master the ability to prioritize. Those priorities depend on timing and where you are in life, Eunice said.

While it is often a woman's instinct to do so, Eunice stressed the need to not try to take care of everybody else. Women too often do this at the expense of taking care of themselves. Eunice learned the hard way that she is the most important one to take care of. "Once you are doing that, it will be easier for you to treat others well. When you treat people well, you actually get something back. It's a very simple formula.

If you can't give it, you obviously won't get it," Eunice explained. Author Hal Runkel talks about the principle Eunice is addressing in his book, Screamfree Parenting. He dedicates a whole chapter to "putting on your own oxygen mask first." If we don't give ourselves the care we need for our own survival, we won't be able to help anyone else.

Chapter Highlights

- For many women, there will be a significant amount of personal sacrifice involved in any major accomplishment. We strive to have it all, but there is always a cost. We can begin to find work/life balance through prioritized choices.

- When you make a list of your priorities, remember to put yourself on it. The better you take care of yourself, the better you can take care of your family and your career.

- None of us does it alone. Ask for help when you need it. Return that help when you can, and there is no reason for guilt.

- Creating a balanced life is your responsibility. Your

boss and your company cannot be expected to give you balance. You have made the choices that have led you to where you are today. You can also choose to change or eliminate some of the things in your life that have caused the scales to tip too far in one direction.

- So many women struggle to find that work/life balance. Talk with others. Seek their counsel. Know that your situation is unique, but you are not alone. Sometimes, just knowing you are in a community of women facing similar issues helps take some of the pressure and stress off.

- Oh, and take a vacation every once in a while. Pamper yourself, and see how everyone around you thanks you for it

Chapter Three
Connecting and Achieving

"The greatest ability in business is to get along with others and to influence their actions."
- John Hancock

I learned my most valuable lesson about the importance of building and nurturing relationships in graduate school at the University of Southern California. I had underestimated the time it would take me to drive the 60 miles from home to class (at their Sacramento campus) and ended up a few minutes late on my very first day. I arrived just as the class was ending the introductions. I had barely gotten into my seat when it was my turn to say who I was, where I worked and where I lived.

Immediately, the professor said, "Oh, you live in the Bay Area, you need to meet Lesa, who also lives in the Bay Area and is looking for someone to carpool to school with on weekends. He then pointed to a woman sitting on the opposite side of the classroom. I was ticked! I was already aggravated at having to go to graduate school (more on that in the next chapter), and then some professor who doesn't even know me has the audacity to volunteer me to carpool with a total stranger. I had already resigned myself to commuting in misery. My class in USC's rigorous graduate program met every weekend in Sacramento. It required class attendance every Thursday through Sunday from 8 a.m. to 5 p.m. This was just something I wanted to get through and move on with my life. I did not know yet how much I would come to value my graduate school experience, or the people I would meet there. At that point, all I knew for sure was my precious family time was being given up, so that I could get the degree I felt I needed to propel my career. I was focused on that and being angry about it. I had no intention of making any new acquaintances.

At the first break, Lesa very cordially came over to me and introduced herself. She remained oblivious to my true attitude about carpooling. Amazingly, I managed to conceal it outwardly. She was in her second year of the graduate program and explained that between tuition and only having a part-time job, the cost of gas every weekend was getting to be a bit of a strain. Swallowing my own selfishness, I offered a meeting location and time for us to connect the next morning. We hit it off and are still friends to this day.

During that first year of commuting, I was able to start sending her job descriptions of available positions at Kaiser. We spent time during our commute discussing the roles, preparation and opportunities that could parlay her current work experience to Kaiser. That year, she secured a full-time position there.

One year later, during our final semester in the graduate program, an excited Lesa called me at work. She told me a friend of hers recently contacted her about an executive search firm conducting a national search for a global director of public policy and communications for Bayer Pharmaceuticals' new biotechnology division, which was being expanded in Berkeley, California. Lesa said to her friend, "That's not my skill set, but I know the perfect person for the job." She gave me the contact information, and I followed up with the firm. That was the beginning of the largest growth phase of my career into biotechnology - both from an acceleration perspective and financial perspective. And to think I almost missed out on this opportunity, because I was not in the mood to make any new friends.

It is a good example, and one I tell often when discussing the importance of relationships in business. Where would I be now if I had let my frustration over graduate school and carpooling get the best of me that day? It is impossible to know for sure, but it is safe to say my path and career opportunities very well could have been different. It is through Lesa that I learned about the opportunity at Bayer. Being kind when I didn't want to be opened up possibilities professionally for me that I couldn't have foreseen. It benefited me professionally, but just as important, or more important than, what this relationship did for my career is what it did for me personally. I made a friend whom I have kept over the years. That is something to be treasured.

So, I would challenge you to never underestimate the value of being nice. Make the choice to be nice to everyone. This seemingly small courtesy sometimes takes effort, like it did for me that first day I met Lesa, but it can pay off in dividends, both personally and professionally. A kind word, a smile or, say, a ride can, somewhere down the road, have an impact on your life, like it did for me. So, whatever challenges you may be facing personally, never let them get in the way of your kindness, of forming new relationships, because these are a foundation of your success in all areas of your life.

Friendship-Based Networking

A former Genentech colleague of mine who had moved on to Elan called me when I was just beginning this book. He was on a mailing list to receive my Power UP newsletter and had just read my most recent edition. This led him to my website and eventually to a phone call with me. He wanted to talk to me about consulting with Elan on a problem they were having. They needed advice from someone with my skill set. He emailed me about the role, and from that contact

I had a series of meetings with various leaders in the company, which resulted in my being offered a senior vice president position there. This is another example of what I like to call friendship-based networking. He was, first and foremost, my friend, not just a network connection, but the relationship benefited my career.

For this reason and others, I prefer using the term 'being nice' rather than 'networking.' I've noticed the two are not interchangeable. Some people who reach out in the name of networking are not genuine. They try to use people to get a job or new business. The gesture toward fostering a relationship, in these cases, is shallow, and the results, if there are any, are often short-term, as is the relationship. People do not like to be used. We do not respond well to being manipulated. That kind of networking more often than not proves to be completely ineffective.

So, if you think in terms of being kind to everyone – as I did with Lesa at USC - then you won't have to worry about whether you are effectively networking. It will naturally flow out of your attitude and approach and will become a much more powerful tool for you. My approach to networking is to make connections that can become lifelong friends – not just pawns to help me get in the door at a new company.

Examples of power connections will be seen throughout the book. Many of the women featured in this book provide examples of powerful connections as a tried and proven method of finding a new job.

Power Up!
Kim Thiboldeaux
President and CEO, The Cancer Support Community
(formerly The Wellness Community and Gilda's Club Worldwide)
Author, The Total Cancer Wellness Guide

When Kim made the decision to join The Wellness Community 10 years ago, there were two staff members and 17 affiliates. The organization was also at a real turning point, which would impact its overall future and sustainability. A decade later, under Kim's leadership, the non-profit organization, now known as The Cancer Support Community, has grown to 25 staff members and 50 affiliates with $35 million in revenue.

Kim credits this success and growth first to a very real focus on and commitment to the mission of providing support for people with cancer and their families. She's never allowed the organization to stray from this idea. This means she and the organization had to maintain the ability to never let egos, distractions or personalities get in the way of moving the mission forward.

Secondly, she credits The Cancer Support Community's success to strong relationships and ongoing relationship building. To meet the needs of cancer patients, Kim and her staff have built relationships with donors, hospitals, cancer centers, government entities and local affiliates throughout the United States and in several other countries. Indeed, Kim has created a multidisciplinary network around the organization with varying layers of support.

"There is an innermost circle of advisers who know the field and who will always help us do the right thing. Beyond that, there are two or three layers of people who provide input on various other areas,"

Kim explained. "We work hard to be a good, reliable, faithful and trusted partner to the various entities that make up our network of relationships. These are commitments we have made as a team, as well as individuals."

According to Kim, in order to build sustainable relationships, it's important to maintain a culture which focuses on the mission, is honest, transparent and functions with dignity and respect. Kim has established core values in the organization of being reliable and responsive. Regardless of the relationship, whether it is a person with cancer, a donor or a hospital, she wants it to be known that they will get a quality product from her organization and a high level of responsiveness. That is what people have come to expect. The Cancer Support Community's success is a direct result of Kim's, and the entire organization's, approach to relationship building.

At the beginning of her career and before moving to the private sector, Kim worked in non-profit healthcare in a community clinic which focused on HIV/Aids. While working at the clinic, she established relationships with staff members from Roche Pharmaceuticals and was asked to come interview for an advocacy relations position in organ transplant and oncology. Initially, she was not interested, but the Roche colleague asked her to do the interview as a favor, promising that there was a lot more there than Kim knew or understood without talking further to the organization.

The colleague's promise proved to be true. Intrigued by the opportunity to fill and define a newly created position, as well as a new department, Kim's own entrepreneurial spirit was fueled. She was willing to take a closer look. The interview went so well that she and her interviewer were finishing each others' sentences by the end of conversation. She began to think that maybe there was something there and that maybe she could use some experience in the private sector – not to mention an increase in her compensation.

Kim went on to accept the Roche position and was fortunate enough to have two great bosses over the next four years. Kim calls it her "on the job" MBA. She learned about business, budget, management, finances and strategy. It proved to be a great experience for her.

During her time with Roche, Kim worked with non-profits, and she eventually realized she wanted back into the non-profit arena. Even after she resolved to return to non-profit work, Kim did not rush into the transition. She stayed at Roche until the right opportunity presented itself.

It finally did present itself during one of Kim's treks out into the community. As part of her job in advocacy relations, she participated in ride-alongs with Roche field representatives. She would visit customers, including physicians and community-based non-profit organizations. She was taken to visit The Wellness Community in Philadelphia and commented that it was a nice local support organization. She was informed that TWC actually consisted of 17 facilities across the nation. To which Kim responded, "Well, you are missing the boat, because no one has heard of you. You need to build your national reputation." She was invited to join the national board and went to every board meeting full of ideas. Finally, she was asked,

"Why don't you just come do it?"

The invitation came at a turning point in her career at Roche, just as the company was talking to her about a global job in Switzerland. It was a great job and position, and she pretended to herself for a while that she was seriously considering it. But she knew in her heart that she would take the TWC job because of the chance to create and build something and fulfill a wonderful mission. "Initially, I said to myself, 'Let me go in for two or three years, get them on a good track and then maybe move on.' Now 10 years later, I am still incredibly excited and enthused by this work," Kim says.

Unfortunately, cancer continues to threaten so many individuals every year. The need and demand to help those people and their families continue to grow. TWC looks for continued opportunities to help more and more of those in need. One recent opportunity was the merger with Gilda's Club, something Kim saw as a way to extend the mission. "Sometimes we are too modest in the non-profit world. No one wants to say, "We want to be the biggest and the best," but, basically, what that means is you're going to be bringing the best you can bring to people with cancer," Kim explains. "It's okay to be the best, because it's a matter of bringing that mission to so many more people. The merger is allowing us to do that."

The merger between Gilda's Club and TWC, which involves integrating organizations and affiliates, has brought up the issues of compromise, relationships and trust. Teams and advisers from both organizations have been brought together, allowing for extensive input from each side. According to Kim, the keys to a successful merger lie in asking the right questions, letting people know they do have a voice in the process and understanding that each voice matters.

You will get as many disparate opinions as there are people in any complex merger. As a leader in that process, Kim says, you have to be willing to make decisions. "A lot of folks are not wiling to take risks, pull the trigger, and live with the consequences," Kim said. "Get good information, have good advisers around you, and then you will gain the confidence and chutzpah needed to make sound decisions."

Kim makes tough decisions, understanding that she and her team will have to live with them. She credits her rapport with her team to the fact that they know she has their backs. She will take responsibility and never throw them under the bus. At the end of the day, they feel good knowing they can trust her, and they are a true team.

Everyone and every team makes mistakes along the way. But worse than making mistakes is not acting at all, something Kim calls "analysis paralysis." "We've made lots of mistakes along the way, but that's how you will learn and grow. We shouldn't be afraid to make mistakes as long as we can grow, make progress, modify our path, and learn. When you have trust, equity, and good relationships, people are a little more forgiving," Kim explains. The only cure for making mistakes is getting back on course.

Relationships and Fun

While trust is essential to successful business relationships, Kim never underestimates what having a little fun can do in building rapport among team members. "While fun may not be the number-one priority in a business relationship, it is nice to connect to people on a human level, find out about their lives and what makes them tick," Kim said. She has learned amazing things throughout the merger and integration of new employees, thanks to relaxing, letting her guard down and having fun with her colleagues.

Kim believes the nature of her work with cancer patients demands fun. "People are going through many character-building opportunities in their lives. Cancer is a very serious illness, and our mission is very serious, so having fun is very important. We must find moments of levity and find humanity during our work. While you should not pry, taking time to show some interest in people's personal life is a strong relationship builder," she says.

Kim has been working in the cancer community for 15 years, 10 of those years in her current role. She knows a lot of people and has a lot of professional relationships. But, she loves that when she sees colleagues at conferences throughout the country, their first question to her is not "What is going on at The Wellness Community?" Instead, they tend to ask, "Where have your travels taken you?" Or they'll ask about her eight nieces and nephews and other family members.

They know to ask these questions, because they know Kim. They know that, besides her work, these are the things that are important to her. They know that travel is part of what defines her, and they know she dotes on the children in her family as much as she can. Kim's business relationships go beyond the surface. She has managed to forge personal relationships with colleagues, and this has helped foster mutual respect. Being able to see other dimensions of a coworker's life, coming to understand what makes them laugh, what motivates them and what their passions are often help create a more harmonious work environment that is based on respect. Each considers the others and who they are outside of the job.

Mentoring

When Kim hears the word "mentoring," she

thinks of intense, long-term mutually-beneficial relationships, not sporadic advice given on-the-go after a meeting by a colleague in management. "I feel, in the non-profit world, we may be at a unique advantage, because we have a board of directors, and to a certain extent, the board have become my mentors and advisers," Kim said. So, Kim estimates she has about 35 advisers.

Over the years, she has had a chance to shape that board, so it is now very diverse with far-reaching knowledge inside and outside of healthcare. "The board is very strategic and not at all a rubber stamp board. I feel questioned, challenged and forced to think and approach work more strategically," Kim explained. "I do not forget, however, that they are also my bosses, and, therefore, I can't go to them with personal issues or job hunting. So, I have a whole separate group of friends and trusted people in my life who I admire and know will challenge me that I go to for more personal mentoring."

Kim wants people around her who are going to help her be the best she can be at everything she does.

"We all have blind spots, so we need reality checks via people who are going to hold us accountable, push us, move us and challenge us at work and personally in ways that we are not able to do on our own. These relationships are important, because I want to be the best human being, best CEO, best aunt and best daughter," Kim said.

Kim believes every woman should have her own board of directors or cabinet team, so to speak. In most companies, everyone does not have access to the board. But, Kim likes to challenge friends and peers to create their own board both inside and outside of the organization. "Maybe women should be looking at this model and create this idea of a board that will point them in the right direction and challenge them, even if they don't have a formal mentoring structure," Kim said. "So, for example, if they have five questions or challenges in a certain area, they know this is who they are going to go to for advice and counsel."

Most people can call to mind friends or colleagues they would choose if creating a personal board of directors. Kim believes in diversity of personality, occupation and outlooks for a successful board. "Even if you have your sights set on one person you admire, you have to recognize that one person, no matter how successful, will not bring all the dimensions you will need to grow, develop and move to the next step. That comes from a diversity of advisers," Kim explained.

Ask Mary

I am trying to maintain a good relationship with my boss, but I am getting increasingly resentful, because I feel I am being overworked. How should I handle this situation, so I do not hurt my place in the company, but I get the results I need to achieve more balance in my life?

I have encountered this question many times over the past couple of years. I believe the reason more and more people are feeling the stress of an increased workload is twofold. In the information age, when almost everyone in every office is a knowledge worker, we're paid to process information. And since there seems to be a nearly infinite amount of information, there's a nearly infinite amount of work. For everyone.

The state of our economy over the past few years has only added to the strain. Many companies have had to lay employees off, delay hiring needed, additional staff or transition employees to part-time status, so they can cut costs and remain viable. Those of you lucky enough to still have your jobs may have had to absorb some extra work and additional responsibilities. All of a sudden, you find your duties overwhelming and your to-do list daunting.

The situation you find yourself in is becoming a common one, especially as many companies remain unable or unwilling to hire more employees until the economy further stabilizes. And as you likely know, the information age has no intention of slowing down. As a result of these truths, you may have to find a solution within the confines of your current position and its revamped description. Don't be disheartened, however, there are several steps you can take to lighten your load and clear the clutter from your mind and your desk.

1. Keep the lines of communication open with your boss

It would not serve you well to go whining to your

boss, who may be feeling the strain as you are, but that is not to say you shouldn't have an open dialogue with him or her. That line of communication is essential to your happiness and satisfaction at the company. A good boss knows this and welcomes your input and conversation. Discuss your challenges without complaining. Ask his or her advice, regarding priorities, but have ideas along those lines yourself first. It is best to go into a conversation with potential solutions in hand. Do not put the work of figuring out your job on your boss. This could diminish his or her confidence in you and your abilities to problem solve. However, going in for a conversation in which you say, "Here's the best path I think we can take in with this project. What do you think?" Well, that's a different story. In that scenario, you are the problem solver, just looking for feedback.

While this might not necessarily diminish your workload, it will show you where your focus should be. Productive conversations with your boss can go a long way toward helping you prioritize your projects. I always find my chaos diminishes when I have a prioritized list in hand, as opposed to multiple projects that all need to get done today.

2. Prioritize and Delegate

Once you have established your priorities for the week or the month or even the quarter, find out which parts of each project need to be completed by you. Once you know this, you will also know which parts can be delegated to people in other departments or throughout your own. Assign or request the help of others early in the process, so pieces of all of your outstanding projects are being worked on by someone at all times. This will give you the opportunity to focus on your major responsibilities for each project.

Remember, you are working to maintain healthy relationships with your boss and others in your company. Always be appreciative of those who assist you. Saying "thank you" or complimenting good work goes a long way toward encouraging colleagues to be happy to help you in the future. Your boss will also see and hear about the ease of working with you. Your leadership and time management skills are an asset here, so use them to get your projects done in a timely matter, building and nurturing relationships along the way.

3. Leave work at work

Major projects often find us burning the midnight oil. We bring our work home, and after putting the kids to bed, we sit at our desks and complete another several hours of work. I am no stranger to this scenario. Anyone hoping to get ahead in business finds themselves in this position on occasion. But in the interest of keeping yourself fresh and at full capacity during the workday, it is best not to make this a habit. When the work is always with us, when we have it at our fingertips day and night, it breeds anxiety. There is always the feeling that you should be working. The result is that we are never fully present with our spouse or our children. We never fully achieve the separation between work and home that we need to have a balanced life.

If your boss is one who likes to text you in the evenings or send you emails in the wee hours of the morning, let him or her know there are certain hours that you reserve for family. Again, most bosses, like you, have lives outside of the office, and understand the need for family time. You may schedule one email check before waking up the kids in the morning, or one voice mail and text messaging check before bed. More than that can be disruptive to your personal time. The idea is to give your brain a break and let it regroup, so you can be more productive when it counts.

4. Take satisfaction in doing your best

Deadlines never go away. You will never fully escape stress, despite putting into practice all of my advice. But your stress will, hopefully, diminish, and you will increase your work/life balance, but we live in an ever-evolving world and workplace. Unforeseen challenges await us, unscheduled meetings call us, and, guess what, today the printer doesn't want to work.

We cannot anticipate all that a day will bring, but we can show up. We can come prepared to work. We can nurture our relationships and accept the tasks before us knowing we are doing our best. Our 'A' game is in place, and there is satisfaction in that. Every project is not going to get finished today, but you have a prioritized plan of action and are optimistic about outcomes. If you can get to this place, you may be able to look at that workload with resolve instead of scorn, and your relationship with your boss will remain a positive and productive one.

Chapter Highlights

- Make the choice to be nice to everyone. Never underestimate the value of being nice. This seemingly small courtesy sometimes takes effort, but it pays off in dividends, both personally and professionally.

- The term 'networking' sometimes carries a negative connotation, because people often use these professional connections to get in the door at a new company or sell a product. Instead use these connections to create life-long friendships.

- Take part in friendship-based networking. Relationships, even professional ones, should be nurtured and grounded in something genuine.

- When you are part of a team, remember every voice matters. There will be as many opinions as people, but everyone deserves to be heard and respected.

- As a leader, you need to be able to make a decision. Once that decision is made, you need to take responsibility for the consequences that may result from it. When you do, your team knows you have their backs and will trust you.

- When your workload overwhelms you, talk with your boss about solutions, then prioritize and delegate.

- Nurture your relationships with your colleagues.

- Bring your 'A' game to work, and be proud of your accomplishments. At the end of the day, this will bring you satisfaction that will outweigh the stress of your job.

Chapter Four

Sustain Your Soul - Protecting Your Spirit/ Activating Your Integrity
"If you're going through hell – keep going"
- Winston Churchill

There are three things I know and accept about myself. I like to win. I focus every day on being happy. And among the reasons I work hard is that I want to leave a legacy. Winning, being happy, leaving a legacy – these are all aspirations that arise from a much deeper place inside of me than just survival instincts for food, clothing and shelter. These aspirations resonate in my spirit - the real me that sustains and keeps me going, even in the roughest of times, even through the hell Churchill alludes to in the quote above. It is important to fortify your spirit, so that you get through adversity, setbacks, delays and obstacles.

One of my favorite books that I use for daily prayer and meditation is Prayers That Avail Much, given to me by a dear friend. In its introduction, it lays out the premise that man (or woman) is a spirit, we have souls and we live in bodies. In order to operate successfully, each of these three facets must be fed properly. The soul or intellect feeds on intellectual food to produce intellectual strength. The body feeds on physical food to produce physical strength. The spirit – the heart or inward person – is the real you. It must feed on spirit food, which is found in the Bible and other inspirational sources in order to produce and develop faith. As we feast upon these truths, we have a fresh mental and spiritual attitude, which also positively impacts our ethics and integrity.

Sustaining Your Spirit

A Proverb in the Bible says "A happy heart is good medicine and a cheerful mind works healing, but a broken spirit dries up the bones." Indeed, often times unhappiness and a lack of the will to win comes from a spirit that has been broken by life's rough patches and disappointments.

No one can succeed with a broken spirit. As a young parent struggling to properly discipline my children, I read a book that talked about the difference between my child's will (i.e. letting them know, "You can't just do whatever you want to do") and her spirit. It is important to teach children morals and ethics, but also important not to break their spirit (i.e. never telling them, "You are bad. You'll never amount to anything. You always mess up everything.") It really made an impression on me, and I am always very careful how I talk to my children, others and myself. It reminded me that what we say greatly affects how others feel and how they behave. At the same time, it reminded me that how I talk to myself, my inner dialogue, affects how I feel and how I behave and react to situations.

Please do not downplay this. You really need your spirit. You must nurture it to keep it activated and functioning properly. You may be in an environment where your spirit gets hammered and challenged every day. Your boss may be the type to openly chastise or reprimand you. Maybe he or she deals in negative reinforcement, exerting power and will like a sword. This behavior can slash at your spirit and puncture

your spirit. Over time, you will feel defeated and sur-
render your spirit to this oppression. You may feel you
are doing what is necessary to succeed in that kind of
environment, but in truth, allowing your spirit to sag
affects your productivity at work and at home. Your
ability to impact any situation becomes compromised
when your spirit is flagging. If this is a situation you
find yourself in, you must find ways to recharge your
spirit each day, so it can sustain your physical body. It
is essential to your success. You must recharge it each
day, so that it can sustain your physical body.

Your spirit will help you stop quitting in the middle of progress. Sometimes we lose patience. We keep
striving toward a goal only to encounter road block after road block along the way. We get tired of the fight.
On these occasions, it seems like the best thing to do
is stop resisting, give in and give up. But, it is our spirit
that tells us to quit whining and buoys us. Sometimes
we have just got to go through difficult times, knowing
that the result is that we'll come out a better person
on the other side. Your spirit instinctively knows that
challenging situations won't stay that way. This ad-

versity is temporary, and it offers us an opportunity. If we rise to the occasion with the help of our spirit, we'll see that adversity makes us more humble, a little more tolerant and a lot more confident.

I do something every day to sustain my spirit. For example, I practice maintaining my happiness every day. I can't have pity parties, because pity won't come any more. Pity says, "I'm not coming, because she's just going to talk herself into being happy and encouraged. I can't get her to dwell on her circumstances, her past, her job, her wallet, her boss, her spouse, or her kids. So, I'm not showing up!" Good riddance, Pity. That's one less naysayer, one less voice of negativity in my ear. A friend of mine plays a song for her children when they're cranky. It's called Pity Party Dance . By the time they finish dancing to the song and doing all the moves, their bad mood is usually gone. We should all find a song that makes us feel like that once in a while.

I have made it my mission to find something to rejoice about even in the midst of my trouble. I know that with this mindset I can never be defeated. This is not just a faith slogan. This is my reality, a code by which I live my life. It isn't always easy, but every day I make the decision to renew the mission. You have to make the decision to be happy every day. No one else can make you happy if you have made the decision to be otherwise. It does not matter what is going on around you, there is always a choice to be made. I choose happiness.

Another way I keep my spirit activated is by keeping a journal. I make a point of writing in it every night and reading from it every morning. This helps me stay focused and motivated. I write down my meditations on scripture, songs and my daily encounters with others. I write about the development, growth and learning I observe in others or myself. I write down dreams and aspirations for myself, my spouse, my children, my company and my career. If the dream is something I have been holding onto for a long time I am careful not to sit thinking I can't do it instead of thinking, I'm still going to do this thing. I have learned the significance of renewing your mind each day. It is a biblical principle that works in every area of life.

Every day I have to get myself mentally prepared to win, and my journal helps me do that.

While reading scriptures or affirmations, I have found it is far more powerful to speak these declarations out loud. Your soul and your mind need to hear what your spirit is saying. Not only that, some things needing to happen in your life are waiting for you to speak to them not just to dream about them but to give voice to them. This is what I did when I began to declare that I would be a senior vice president even when there was no job in sight. This practice is born out every day by the women participating in the Women's Health Initiative described in the Chapter 7 Power Up profile. A major objective (and hurdle) of the program is to convince participants to verbalize every day what their dreams are.

Daily, I declare scriptures or affirmations over my spouse, my children, my staff, my extended family, my day and myself. As I meditate and am struck by particular scriptures or desires for myself or others, I write them down.

About once per quarter, I type up a new page of

them. I keep copies in my car and near my bed, so I can access them daily. I find it better to have a one- or (at the most) two-page copy to meditate on for a few months at a time. This helps me become grounded in some strong principles before I move on to another set. I call this getting in the zone for utmost performance. If I take a haphazard approach and randomly make declarations, I almost get the performance I want that day. If I keep the same set ad infinitum, that is the most I'll ever learn, and my performance will become stagnate and rote. If I refresh my meditations every few months, I am continually developing and achieving utmost performance.

Listening and dancing to powerful music is another way that I sustain my spirit. I am very careful what I listen to and what I look at. I don't listen to depressing, whining music. You are correct if you are hearing a theme here. Anyone who has ever worked for or with me knows I have zero tolerance for whining. Back in the days when I grew up, we used to get spankings. I was never a kid who got the whiner's spanking. I could never understand my cousins who kept crying even after the spanking was over –to the point of aggravating the parent so much they spanked them again to make them be quiet. I never saw anyone get a spanking and somehow get it undone or stop the pain by whining. Even as a child, I thought to myself, 'Suck it up!'

In the same way, I don't understand whining songs. Singing about the love you lost is not going to bring them back. My advice? Shut up and sing about something else. Okay, that's my vent. I like to hear joyful, encouraging, inspiring songs. It is no wonder that inspirational and gospel music sales as well as inspirational books outsell all other types of books and music. They make us feel better. They lift us up. They put us in a place where we feel we can achieve something, be successful. After you hear the "somebody done somebody wrong" song on your way to work, you will be ready to "go off" on the first person that says something to you the wrong way. I am telling you, it makes a difference. What we hear affects us. It can set the tone for our day, creating an inspiring positive mood or a dark, negative one.

One of my favorite classes in graduate school at the University of Southern California was Organizational Development. It was my favorite, not only because it helped me understand the psyche of companies, but, even more importantly, it helped me understand the psyche of people like me, people who have made the decision to dedicate their career and, thereby, a major part of their lives to a corporation or industry. There are two discussions from that class that have always stuck with me. One of the memorable conversations dealt with trying to keep people happy in the workplace, and the other with the concept of legacies.

In one robust discussion about employee happiness, the younger members of the class found themselves at odds with the older members of the class. My younger classmates felt strongly (well, frankly, they insisted) that companies and supervisors should do everything possible to make employees happy. My older classmates (okay, I must include myself in this group, so let's say, the more mature group rather than older) and I disagreed. We felt corporate leaders should not worry about making employees happy.

Our instructor, in obvious amusement, let the debate continue for a period of time. Eventually the debate wound down to me, a voice of experience and maturity, and another young woman, Diane. She passionately pointed out how people are dedicating their lives and time to a company. She argued that anyone wanting to be a good manager could indeed make employees happy, if they really cared and tried hard enough. She looked at all of us (old coots in her mind, I imagine), and in a 'shame on you' tone, said, "When I become a manager, I am going to make sure all of my staff are happy."

There was total quiet in the room. When I could no longer stand it, I took a deep breath, and in my most respectful and measured tone, said, "I agree that managers should try to make the work experience enjoyable for employees. But if you talk to managers who have been managers for some time, they will tell you that there are some people who will never be happy – no matter what or how much you do for them. They have made up their minds that they will not be satisfied. They are eternal complainers. They will just keep you jumping to try to please them, and it will never be enough."

At this point, the instructor interjected and said my position was absolutely correct. Some people are just never going to be happy no matter what.

I could see Diane and her team mulling this over and realizing that happiness is not totally in the managers' control. "Okay," Diane nodded, looking at me and in an admonishing tone continued, "But you agree that managers should at least try?" "Absolutely," I responded.

When I am mentoring women who tell me they are not happy in their jobs, I am quick to remind them that they are solely responsible for their own happiness. Neither their boss nor their company, nor their spouse or kids can force them into happiness. It's up to them.

Sustaining Your Soul

Our soul feeds on intellectual food, so we must continue to educate ourselves, expand our knowledge and nurture our mind and capacity to learn. It is not enough, however, to fill our heads with random bits of information about this or that. We should educate ourselves with purpose.

Wherever you go in life or whatever you set out to do, you must move toward that place with a purpose in mind. Without a direction or focus, you will never get where you want to go. Think of a car's navigation system. It is only useful when you type in where you are going. Without a set destination, it is of no use to you. In the same way, we need a destination, a goal, in mind, so we can educate and prepare ourselves for our arrival at that place. If your career advancement is the goal, then every turn along the path should take you closer to your ultimate job or position within a company. Chart your course with a definite goal in mind, and you are more likely to achieve that goal.

When plotting your course, or setting out your career goals, think about the highest possible achievement for yourself professionally. What would be the ultimate job for you? What position within your organization or your dream organization, do you most desire? Even if it seems unattainable, even if it seems so impossible it's laughable, make this your goal. Your goals should always be set beyond what you believe is attainable. When you dream small, you make very small advances. When you dream big, you make medium-sized advances. But, when you dream the impossible (or at least what you might feel is the impossible), you advance in big, amazing ways, personally and professionally.

You will surprise others with your determination and clarity of purpose. But, your achievements will not surprise you, because you dreamed them, you wrote them down, and by doing that, you made them part of your realm of possibility. You made attaining those seemingly impossible dreams possible. By writing your fantasy job on paper, you transformed it into a goal. You gave direction and a final destination to your internal navigation system.

During the time I was completing my final graduate course at USC - the Capstone course - taught by Professor Bob Myrtle, I was also recruited to work for Bayer Corporation's Global Biotechnology unit in

Berkeley. It was my first director position, and I eagerly shared the news about the promotion with Dr. Myrtle.

"Guess what," I beamed, "I just got offered a new job in a Director-level position!" Without skipping a beat, he said, "Of course you did, and when you get a call in two years for that vice president position, it will be even more exciting." I just smiled at him and kept walking, but inside I distinctly remember thinking, "Vice President? What in the world is he talking about?" The thought of a vice president position had never dawned on me. I couldn't really revel too much in achieving the Director level position, because I realized he had just hung out a new carrot. So, I immediately took note of, and latched on to, his total confidence that this bigger opportunity would happen.

I knew, from my years of nurturing my spirit and developing my intellect, that I had to be proactive in not losing sight or hope of that possibility. I wrote about it in my journal that night, regularly meditated on it and started declaring (talking about) it. As I mentioned in Chapter Two, I told my children about it, and they helped keep me on track, exercising my faith for this by regularly asking me if I was promoted to vice president.

All of this helped me set my expectations higher than I imagined when I enrolled in graduate school. I realized that all I had to do was keep up a steady intellectual diet for my soul and keep moving on my path. Eventually, I did attain a vice president position as my professor predicted. I did not need any outside reinforcement or prodding when it was time for me to raise my expectations to senior vice president. The desire for the position, and the ability to attain it were already in me. My professor had only made me aware of them.

Sustaining Your Integrity

Our desire to improve our character and do the right thing reflects our commitment to ethics and integrity. One of the reasons this is so important is because we are all mindful of how we want to be remembered. Whether it is with our family, at a company, or in a neighborhood, we all have a desire to leave a strong positive legacy.

Anyone who knows me well will tell you I like action movies. Watching an intense, action-packed film is one of my favorite ways to wind down and relax. If there is no car chase or fight scene in the first five or 10 minutes of the movie, I'm ready to go home. I like suspenseful movies with the good guys and the bad guys going head to head to come up with new and heart-stopping ways to win.

To illustrate the desire for legacy, I'll use an example from one of my favorite action movies, Transformers, starring Shia LaBeouf as Sam Witwicky and Megan Fox as Mikaela Banes. There is one scene fairly early on in the movie in which the two main characters find themselves at a crossroads. Sam and Mikaela have just witnessed a major fight between the good guys' (autobots) car and the bad guys' (deceptacons) car. The autobots are lying on the ground, where they have fallen in exhaustion after running from the deceptacons and are looking at the two transformed cars in a vicious fight. The autobot temporarily overpowers the deceptacon long enough to convert back to a car, pulls up to Sam and Mikaela and opens the door. Sam says, "It wants us to get in." An incredulous Mikaela, who is still overwhelmed by the fact that she was almost killed (not to mention seeing a car transform into a robot warrior and back), says, "I'm not getting in there." Sam looks at her and says, "Fifty years from now, don't you want to be able to look back over your life and say you had the guts to get in the car?"

That's my favorite scene in the movie. It speaks to my innate desire to matter, to make a difference, to leave a mark. Of course, our heroine accepts the challenge. The two characters get in the car and eventually save the world. His appeal to her desire for legacy helped her overcome fears, misgivings and uncertainty about the outcome.

Everybody wants to leave a legacy. One of the reasons we want power and progress is because we want to leave a legacy. Throughout the rest of my life, I want to be able to look back and say I had the guts to get in the car. I had the guts to go for that new job, to go back to school, to take the shot, to go for that promotion, to re-enter a promise (as mentioned in bullet

#5 below). I want my children and family to know that about me as well.

We all have been blessed with natural as well as learned gifts and talents. The Bible says your gifts will make room for you and bring you before great and mighty men.

Developing your spirit and feeding our soul facilitates the development of your character. Your gift defines your potential and your character determines your legacy. In other words, your gift will get you to a place of power and achievement in life, but your character will keep you there.

In the same organizational development class where I debated about employee happiness, I participated in another interesting discussion about legacy. This discussion revolved around how to handle the fast-approaching retirement of an important executive. In this scenario, the company had already named a replacement for the exiting executive. With this new executive, the company was planning a new focus and direction, but it still really needed the exiting executive to transfer the knowledge and skills he had attained over the years to assure the success of his re-placement.

My instructor asked class members to take shots at having hypothetical conversations with the retiree. How would class members approach the retiree about offering his time to train or advise his successor? Our mock meetings with the retiree were enlightening, to say the least. The first class member to volunteer decided it would be best to meet with the retiring executive and, during that meeting, remind him he was getting a generous retirement package. Next, the class member proceeded to let the executive know he needed to make sure he did a good job with the transition. In other words, the idea was to intimidate him into cooperating with his replacement.

Not one to stay in the background for long, I asked to take the next shot at the retiree. My dialogue with him went something like this: "Joe, you have been a valuable employee to this company – a stalwart really. You have facilitated some of our most successful processes and platforms and invested a significant part of your life to our success. After all the hard work you have done, I know you want to see the company continue to grow and succeed on even more levels. As you know, Bill has been charged with merging your operation and his, ideally to build an even stronger enterprise and platform. Assuring the successful integration of your operation with his before you retire provides an ideal opportunity for you to leave an even greater legacy."

After my first sentence, my professor began nodding his head and making a circular motion with his hand indicating for me to continue, continue. When I finished, he explained why my dialogue would be successful. People have a strong desire to leave a legacy, he said. Money may not entice them; titles may not entice them, but the opportunity to be remembered and to still be making a contribution even after they have moved on to other endeavors is the strongest motivation of all. This is a character-building trait.

Of course, when you get on the subject of character, you can't overlook honesty, integrity, fairness, kindness, helpfulness, self-control and forgiveness. Interestingly, many of these traits are also listed in the

Bible as fruits of the Spirit. If you nurture your spirit, ethics and integrity will be a natural product in your life. You'll be a "good guy."

I especially like movies where the good guys win. Good guys help make the world a better place. Like everyone else, even in this exponentially accelerated world, I want to make a positive impact in as many areas as I can. I like to win. I don't get up in the morning thinking, "Oh, I think I'll lose ground today." I get up every morning wanting to win. Winning to me means making progress. I get up every day with a mindset to make progress toward achieving my goals – with a mindset to do whatever is necessary (with integrity) to keep advancing.

Acquire the Tools and Wisdom to Overcome Challenges

There are negative forces that we have to be wary of and steel ourselves against in order to overcome. I wrote my first book, 10 Keys to Overcoming Disappointment, to help people achieve the ability to deal with things that don't change – matters of the heart, emotional turmoil and adversity. To be successful, we must all develop the ability to deal with the facts of life that impact us every day – the marriages and relationships that failed, elusive career goals, loss of a loved one, material losses – all of those things that just didn't work out the way we had hoped or expected. No matter how successful we are, there will always be these unexpected setbacks. We all have to navigate emotional landmines that are buried along our paths.

This is why among all of our important "acquisitions," which include knowledge, possessions, and accolades, we must also acquire the wisdom and tools to help us overcome the rough patches in life. There are a few key things you can do, a few tools you can employ, that will make you better able to move forward and overcome life's various adversities.

1. We must learn to forgive, and let go of the past. Being able to do this frees you. A burden you have been carrying will be gone, and once your load is lightened, the future seems brighter, possibilities increase, and happiness can grow.

2. You must accept that there is no substitute for allowing the grief process to run its course. When

you have suffered a big loss of any kind, you need time to work through the barrage of emotions you will face as a result. Be patient with yourself. There is no quick fix. It is a process, and you will come out the other side eventually.

3. We must face our fears and keep striving for greatness in spite of them. Fear is the biggest obstacle to our success. Be conscious of it. When you identify what scares you and why, you can begin to move through it. It may never go away completely, but it can diminish with work. Education and confidence in your abilities help you take an overwhelming, debilitating fear and turn it into a quiet (though maybe still nagging one) that you can ignore. I have found that the only way to totally eradicate this type of fear is to face it head on and do the thing that is frightening you so that you realize it can never stop you unless you let it.

4. We must engage our indomitable spirit. It always stands at the ready to help us go just one step further and will never allow us to quit or accept defeat. It is defiant against all odds. Spiritual comfort will always be available to us whether through prayer,

meditation or reading the Bible, and we can sometimes derail ourselves if we are moving too fast to take
advantage of it.

5. We can re-enter the promise of our dreams
and purpose that disappointment tried to steal. Those
goals that you wrote down and meditated on? Don't
give up on them just because you had setbacks. Setbacks, interruptions to our long-term goals, are a part
of life. We all go through them. The difference comes in
how we handle our disappointments. If you can come
through them having learned something that can positively impact your future, you haven't lost anything.
Resurrect the dream and begin again.

My first marriage ended in divorce. I had to
make the decision to trust again, love again and re-enter the promise of marriage and relationship. My first
child died of a crib death at two months old. At first,
I vowed never to have another child. I couldn't bear
the thought of experiencing such terrible loss again.
But I refused to stay parked in that place of grief and
mourning. I had to tap into a stronger power source of
prayer and healing and re-enter the promise of moth-

erhood. And now, three children later, am I ever glad I did!

We must stay in a state of expectancy, meaning we must always expect things to get better. We must be vigilant in seeking the opportunity that will make all the difference to us. We must believe that that opportunity is coming. Some people call this optimism, or positive thinking, but it can also be called faith. And it's important. Supplement that faith with prayer, and you are well on your way. Once we learn to navigate our spiritual and emotional "landmines," we can continue to move forward with our life and accomplishments.

Power Up!

Mary Cranston,

Firm Senior Partner

Pillsbury Winthrop Shaw Pittman

When Mary Cranston graduated from law school, she went to work for an old, established law firm. She was a good associate and always in demand at the firm, but there came a time when Mary realized she wanted more for herself and her career than just being a part of someone else's execution team. She wanted to try her own cases, big ones.

After some reflection, Mary realized what she wanted was to become a trial lawyer, defending big companies in high-stakes court cases. She looked around for someone to emulate, a woman who had charted the same path who could mentor her. The problem was that there were no other women in her field at that time doing what she wanted to do. Rather than give up and make the choice to stay where she was, Mary made the decision to mentor herself instead.

No female mentor existed, but that did not mean Mary couldn't chart her own course based on her research, experience and goals. She first determined what skills she would need to transition herself into a trial attorney. She then identified what achievements would make it clear she had achieved her goal.

Mary often visualized herself in the role she hoped to adopt one day. She pictured herself in court, with lot of money on the line for a company. She also pictured herself in a boardroom wielding a lot of power.

During all of her goal-setting and visualizing, Mary admits to being afraid. She feared she couldn't do it, and that even if she could, the legal culture wasn't ready for the realization of her dreams. Fortunately, she understood her fears were not irrational. She was not just being paranoid. There certainly were indicators in the marketplace that this might not be doable.

So, Mary's fears sat in the forefront of her mind. She did not try to repress them, but neither did she focus on them. "I just patted them on the head and moved towards my dreams and goals. I realized you cannot make them go away, but you don't have to invest in them with huge amounts of energy," Mary said. She allowed a part of her mind to observe them and kept the other part of her mind focused on where she wanted to go.

For five years Mary worked toward her goal. At the end of that time, her dream was realized. Mary became a very well-known trial attorney. "There is a huge amount of power available to everyone," Mary realized through her journey. "Free your mind to go out there, and find power for each new vision step by step."

Mary's journey also taught her the path she chose was not for the weak of heart. She had to get out of her comfort zone, face her fears or fail. "To be different, you have to think differently. You have goals that are different and have to get out of your comfort zone. Change is inevitable. Are you going to have positive change or a shrinking inward focus? Change is going to happen. That is one thing you can't stop."

Mary believes sustaining her spirit and soul were crucial elements to her success. She worked hard to train her mind, so she could use it as a tool versus an obstacle during her five-year journey to become a trial attorney. She refused to let her mind, often filled with fear, run the show. "So many people are run by their minds, and they have constant repeating thoughts - repetitive thoughts that are not necessarily productive ones bouncing around. You have to find a part of yourself that's not your thought pattern," Mary explained.

Mary escaped her looping thoughts and liberated her mind by meditating every day for five years. "When you can attain those states where your mind calms down, you can access higher power and a lot of energy. Prayer can achieve that result, and so can various forms of physical exercise," Mary said. "These calming exercises can even improve your immune system, so you can use them for your mind, body, and spirit."

These days Mary regularly uses meditation to improve her work. Before writing a law brief, she takes 15 minutes to meditate. This helps her get rid of negative or unproductive thoughts and come back to a clearer, newer mindset. Through meditation, she achieves new ways of looking at and thinking about situations. She has gotten a reputation for getting briefs done in an amazingly short amount of time. She attributes this ability to her empowering moments during meditation. "You can think in a different way, so you are more calm and peaceful," Mary said. For Mary, having a clear, fresh perspective has helped contribute to her success as an attorney.

When it comes to both her personal and professional lives, Mary likes to remember one of Albert Einstein's famous quotes: "We can't solve problems by using the same kind of thinking we used when we created them." Einstein understood that we have to go to a higher power when looking for solutions. For Mary, that higher power can be found through meditation and prayer. "You can use prayer and meditation to control your mind, thoughts and emotions, so you can achieve a more expanded state of mind. While in this state, you'll find that everything has changed, and there is a new set of thoughts that are more illuminating. You'll find that solution Einstein was talking about," Mary said.

Although Mary has made meditation and prayer a part of her daily life and looks forward to it every day, for a long time she had to consciously remind herself to keep doing these things. It took time out of her day, and it wasn't always easy to get to that place of calm in the midst of the chaos of her life. "It's a discipline, like lifting weights. You have to practice," she said. So, for a while, she was working to become proficient in the art of meditation, and eventually, her diligence paid off. And meditation began working for her. She was quicker at work, could read situations better, and felt more focused. "Your thoughts become less focused on your fears and more on your greater self – that part of you that does believe you are unlimited and does believe you are empowered."

If you're going through hell

Chapter Five
You can Do More Than You Think You Can – Doing the Change Dance
"The path from dreams to success does exist. May you have the vision to find it, the courage to get into it."
-Astronaut Kalpana Chawla

It's 5:00 Monday morning, and your weekday routine begins. You yawn, stretch and roll out of bed. Still tired, you find your way to the bathroom for a quick shower, and then you get dressed for work. Next, you wake up the kids, get them dressed as quickly as possible, and by a miracle from God, corral everyone into the car by 6:45 a.m. for the ride to the daycare or school, where the kids will eat breakfast.

Your car, of course, knows its way to your favorite drive-through, where you get some coffee and a pastry you can eat while stuck in morning rush-hour traffic. In-between bites of food and sips of expensive coffee, you (illegally) use your smart phone to check voice mail and e-mail. All of this before you even set foot into the office – where there's a full day of back-to-back meetings and an impossible "to-do" list waiting for you.

IT e-mails you to let you know that a new system is coming, and training is mandatory. HR wants everyone at the next Employee Benefits meeting, and there's a posting for a cool new job you'd really like to go after. But with the constant swirl of change spinning around you, how will you ever be able to keep your head above water – let alone move ahead?

Does any of the above sound familiar? That's how my days used to go before I realized I would never achieve the control or satisfaction I was seeking until I made some adjustments and got organized. Here's a better approach for the new you – the one that has read this book and is now living a life emanating power, progress and priorities. Ready? See if you feel this might be a better way to start the day.

Your morning routine begins with some quiet time for meditation and mental preparation for the day. You jot down your thoughts for what you want to achieve today, noting the mindset you will need to meet the day's challenges at home and at work. You include meditation and thoughts about how you can help the rest of your household have a fruitful day as well. And just before you rush out into your day, you take just a few more minutes, close your eyes and dream about your future, imagining what will be the next steps for you, your family and your career. You jot down whatever thoughts you have about achieving those dreams as well.

In your plans for the day, you have identified a time to get at least half an hour of exercise. You either do that in the morning or at a set time later in day.

You check your smart device to make sure your schedule has not changed from when you checked it or reviewed it with your assistant before you left the office yesterday.

After you shower and dress, you wake up your kids and get them dressed. You head into the kitchen to prepare a quick hot breakfast of oatmeal or Malt-O-Meal. While water is boiling for the cereal, you pull out a container with cut up fresh cantaloupe, strawberries, pineapple, and grapes. You pop whole grain bread into the toaster for everyone. In 10 minutes, you have a healthy breakfast of hot cereal and fresh fruit to give everyone the physical stamina they will need for the busy day ahead. Also lined up by every dish is today's multi-vitamin always kept on the counter as a reminder.

You get the kids loaded into the car for the drive to school, and on the way you chat with them about their friends, the upcoming day, and what to expect after school.

You get to the office, and the materials for your first meeting are on your desk – either printed by you or your assistant the day before. The first and last item on your schedule is a half hour prep time to review meeting notes, practice for a presentation or make phone calls. Every item on your "to do" list is scheduled on your calendar – whether it's reading a report, participating in a training, having a one-on-one conversation with a team member, or researching a new job. Personal notes like paying the kids' tuition, making a medical or dental appointment or buying a gift are also on you calendar.

Your boss pops in to your office to let you know

an issue is bubbling and a meeting has been scheduled for the afternoon. You quickly realize this meeting will likely run over your scheduled departure, so you contact one of your alternative transportation sources – spouse, another mom or a daycare provider – to get your kids to an after-school practice.

Sounds too good to be true? You can do it if you make a point of scheduling some time every day to get organized so that you think through and plan how your next day or even better, your next week and work will flow. Getting organized includes taking a few moments at the beginning of the week to check in with members of your support system to see what they have coming up this week as well so that you know who to call for help if necessary.

Change is All Around Us

We are living in exponential times. Technology is driving not only how we communicate, but how we live, play, work and entertain – even how we date, establish relationships and take care of our families.

These exponential times are also driving how we

educate and develop ourselves. Staying the same is not an option – not on a personal level and certainly not on a professional level.

Typical responses to change – and why you can't fight it

Staying abreast of the latest technologies is just one part of effectively managing change. As the competitive landscape evolves more and more rapidly for companies and its leaders, it is not uncommon to see companies undergoing transformation efforts to gain or maintain a leadership position. Even more noticeable is the fact that these transformation initiatives are reoccurring ever three to five years. Why? Because new technologies and products, new business models, consolidations, globalization and a dynamic workforce are constantly disrupting even the best laid strategic plans

While you may have the awareness of the need to change as well as the desire to change, if you don't possess the knowledge and the ability to change, you will still get let behind. Or worse yet, you may never realize the fulfillment of your life and career ambitions.

As you identify competencies for your Personal Development Plan, without a doubt Managing Change should be on the list of core competencies necessary for your success. Ideally it will be listed as a strength, but if it is listed as an area for development, it should definitely be a priority.

It is always a good idea to do a regular assessment of your current status and determine if you're still on track to achieve your goals. Have your goals changed? Has your role changed? Are their disrupting factors on the horizon? If so, what are you doing to mitigate them or get in front of them? Is your team still focused on the right things? Do you need to prepare them for changes on the horizon? Are prepared to lead a transformation initiative?

These are just a sample of questions you should regularly ask yourself annually or, given the exponential pace of changes in technology and rapid competitive evolution, do so on a quarterly basis.

It is quite prudent to do some research on change management systems like Prosci's ADKAR to help prepare yourself mentally and professionally to step up to the "change challenge" at any point in your career.

To help yourself better understand your potential reactions to change, take advantage of a personality profile assessment like Insights or Myers-Briggs so that you set yourself and others up for success when change is required.   Not only do you need to understand the potential for self-inflicted pitfalls that may blindside you, but you also need to understand how to parlay your strengths and that of others to assure a successful transition for yourself, your team and your company.

Change means to grow, to arise from what you once were and become what you always hoped or intended to be. Regularly ask yourself, "what am I doing right now to assure that I change through ongoing personal and professional development?"

Human nature being what it is, I already know what you want at this moment. You want a guarantee that if you do everything right, you'll be able to succeed and at some point you can rest on your laurels. While there are no such guarantees in this new rulebook of change, if you are confident, prepared and proactive, you will have a great impact and can achieve much in this exciting and richly rewarding future. The truth is you can do more than you think you can. One thing is for sure, if you don't learn how to grow through change, your progress will be hampered and your dreams delayed or never realized.

True some things are constant – like taxes, life and death. But change is also a constant in life. So, isn't it time you embraced it and used it to your advantage?

Embrace change. Like a good dance partner, go with the flow and enjoy the interesting new twists, turns and places it takes you. Your success and your future lie *within* change – not *against* it.

Power Up!

Dr. Marianne Legato

Professor of Clinical Medicine, Columbia University, College of Physicians and Surgeons

Adjunct Professor of Medicine, Johns Hopkins

Author, Why Men Never Remember and Women Never Forget

Internationally-known academic, physician, author and lecturer, Dr. Marianne Legato created a unique career path for herself, one that is almost as anomalous now as it was in her early days as a doctor. A 1962 graduate of New York University College of Medicine, she spent her early career doing research on the structure and function of the cardiac cell. Her work was supported by the American Heart Association and the National Institutes of Health. And for that work she won a coveted Research Career Development Award from the National Institutes of Health. She was also part of the National Heart Lung and Blood Institute's study section on cardiovascular disease as well as on the Basic Science Council of the American Heart Association. In 1992 she won the American Heart Association's Blakeslee Award for the best book on cardiovascular disease written for the lay public.

While her work in the area of cardiac medicine continues to be honored and respected, Dr. Legato's eventual studies of the new science of gender-specific medicine would come to define her career. At the forefront of the investigation into the science of how normal human function and the experience of the same disease vary as a function of gender, Dr. Legato collaborates with scholars around the world. She strives to advance the science of the differences between men and women. She has founded and directs the Partnership for Gender-Specific Medicine at Columbia University and the Foundation for Gender-Specific Medicine, Inc.

Still in its infancy in many ways, gender-specific medicine continues to navigate breakthroughs, making it a breeding ground for rapid change. After first making tremendous inroads in the area of women's health, Dr. Legato has turned to men's health. She is constantly writing, lecturing and talking to colleagues about gender-based medicine, so that advances continue to be made in this very important approach to practicing medicine. Dr. Legato recognizes her specialty has inadvertently made her an agent of change, rapid change at that, in the medical field.

A pioneer in her own right, Dr. Legato credits much of her success, including her innovation and adaptability, to the pioneer who mentored her through medical school and beyond. Dr. Legato met Dr. M. Irené Ferrer, a ground-breaker in the area of cardiac medicine, while a student at the Columbia University College of Physicians and Surgeons. Dr. Ferrer, one of the country's first women cardiologists, became the first female chief of medicine during World War II, while many male physicians were fighting in the war. It was through Dr. Ferrer's careful mentoring that Dr. Legato successfully completed her medical degree. When financing the remainder of her medical education became a problem for Dr. Legato, Dr. Ferrer visited the dean at the New York University College of Medicine on her behalf and even paid Dr. Legato's tuition fees herself.

In her own career, Dr. Ferrer helped develop

the cardiac catheter. And while Dr. Ferrer's work and career path deserve study, Dr. Legato says her mentor and role model provided her with as much valuable information about what not to do in her career as what to do. Because it was customary during the 50s and 60s, Dr. Ferrer was more acquiescent to the male doctors for whom she worked. As a result she did not get credit for the stunningly innovative work she did in cardiology, according to Dr. Legato. The male doctors with whom she worked received the Noble Prize in 1963 for the development of the catheter. While it was Dr. Ferrer who told the doctors what to do with the Nobel Prize-winning instrument, she was merely mentioned in the doctors' acceptance speech, something she tells Dr. Legato she was delighted about at the time.

Though times have changed and Dr. Ferrer would likely get recognition for such a discovery today, the situation did not sit well with Dr. Legato, who vowed to never be put in the position of not getting credit for her work. Her pre-defined notion of women's worth in medicine caused her to develop a career unique for its innovation more than anything. She went around issues instead of trying to fight them, never asking for permission, if she could avoid it. Instead, she just did what she thought was important, always thinking of herself as a lone ranger. The result of her independence of mind and method was a new specialty, gender-specific medicine. "Do what your mind and heart dictate and never mind asking people what they think. If you think it's right, go do it, even if it ruffles feathers," Dr. Legato said when asked about what advice she would give other potential pioneers.

Another piece of advice Dr. Legato can't help but share pertains to education. She was always very determined about continuing her education, from her initial medical school training to her work in academic medicine, which, by its very nature, requires lifelong education and interaction with global colleagues. She believes in the power of continual study, through which everyone in their chosen fields can come to a place of discovery and pioneering moments. She continues to be stimulated by her colleagues and the environment at Columbia as well as her patients.

Each facet of her work interests Dr. Legato and fosters her learning. While she is committed to her academic work, she finds her interaction with patients the most fulfilling and important work she's ever done. Early on in her career, Dr. Legato was discouraged from going into clinical practice by Dr. Ferrer, who thought she would be most productive in a wholly academic environment. "Dr. Ferrer told me she was opposed to me leaving the lab. She told me, 'You will never be as successful in practice as you have been in the laboratory. You have been brilliant there, and you should stay there,'" Dr. Legato remembered. "But having a mentor should not preclude you from having your own mind and charting your own course."

Like most of the women profiled in this book, Marianne had to figure out ways to mentor herself on occasion. One of the ways she did this was to watch everyone who was successful and imitate them. She even went so far as to rehearse speeches and make terrific slides based on what she saw that was most successful. She also learned how to be charming – not abrasive – which she says is very important (See chapter 8 on fatal flaws). Dr. Legato made a point of always using data, rather than passionate arguments, to convince colleagues of what she was asking them to believe. Finally, if she encountered problems, she asked for their help rather than challenging them.

Marcela Perez de Alonso
Executive Vice President
Human Resources, Hewlett Packard

Marcela Perez de Alonso has reinvented herself several times throughout her life and career. Growing up in Punta Arenas, Costa Rica, she learned early on how the ability to change and adapt would allow her to meet life's opportunities head-on. As a young woman, she made the decision to leave her family and country to pursue a university degree in Santiago, Chile. "It was not an easy thing to do at the time," Marcela explained, "but it turned out to be a pivotal point in my journey."

Shortly after her graduation from Catholic University in Chile, Marcela began working in human resources for a start-up operation. "I started out as a recruiter then moved on to be the division head of HR for the start-up operation, which today is one of the largest banks in Chile," Marcela said. She later went to work for Citibank, where she held several senior-level roles in both operations and human resources, including the lead HR role for Citibank's Global Consumer Business, which at the time was a 100,000-employee organization where Marcela was responsible for developing a host of breakthrough initiatives. During her tenure at Citibank, Marcela also accepted an opportunity in line management to broaden her business experience and expand her knowledge base. In 2004, she joined Hewlett Packard as executive vice president of human resources.

Throughout her career Marcela has lived in several different countries—Mexico, Puerto Rico and, for the last 17 years, the United States, where she has resided in New York, Miami and now California. She's learned to speak English, something she couldn't do before going to work for Citibank. She has moved, immersed herself in language and expanded her education to meet the challenges of her career. Rather than frighten her, however, these changes and her ability to adapt to them have continued to inspire and motivate Marcela.

She considers herself a risk taker. "The most important thing, every time you take a risk and change something (whether it be a company or a city) is to get totally re-energized. Being successful in one place gives you energy for the next challenge," she believes. Marcela advises others to take advantage of the opportunity to combine risk taking with learning about yourself in a certain environment. Then, she says, you are able to use this knowledge to push yourself to the next level. As a general rule, after at least four years in one workplace, Marcela starts looking around and asking what's next. She feels this need for change is a fundamental part of her nature

Marcela does admit change is not free of consequences. There is always the pain of losing things that make you comfortable. "You have to rebuild comfort every time, and it's tough, but each time you have to rebuild, it's easier the next time around," she said.

Marcela feels that with change should come personal as well as professional learning – always giving you the sense you are growing. Celebrating successes is part of the learning and growing process, but so is taking heed of the things that didn't go well. This kind of constant evaluation is important. "I am always looking at what I could have done better, whether that be in my personal life, with my kids or in my career," Marcela said. "Every time I do something new I learn what I will repeat and what I will have the mental discipline to do better next time. If I face a similar situation again, I will know how to handle it better."

Marcela acknowledges that some people are very adverse to change and afraid of change, but she views change as opportunity. It keeps her empowered, energized and focused on what's next. She attributes her comfort with change to experience. "The first change in life is usually uncomfortable, but then the more you change and move forward the more comfortable you become. Experience adds value in the change process. It's a journey, through which you become more comfortable with and about yourself," Marcela said.

Now married to her second husband, Marcela

remembers when she was initially divorced from her first husband and had to raise her children as a single parent. That change was one she found very difficult and a challenge to navigate through. Eventually, she said the change became a positive one. "After a certain amount of time, everything goes in the right direction, and you do things to make it better for your kids, you grow and you feel better about yourself," she said.

Marcela and her second husband of 16 years have found success as a dual-career couple with an atypical living arrangement. He has his own life and work in Miami, while Marcela works in California. Essentially, they have a commuter marriage. At different times, each has moved for career-related reasons, and as a result, there have been times when they did not live together. While this kind of arrangement does not work for every couple, Marcela and her family have found it works well for them. "The key to success in all of the moves we make around the country is making concessions, so everybody enjoys and is happy with our current situation," Marcela explained. "With my husband in Miami during the week and me in California, we get to have a honeymoon every weekend. It also gives both of us a lot of freedom and independence to do what we need to do for our companies during the week."

While moving around the country and succeeding in a commuter marriage works for Marcela, she is often asked by colleagues and friends how they can navigate these same paths as well as she has. One particular question that pops up again and again - How do you build a new network for yourself and your family when you move from one city to another? Marcela urges everyone to tap into neighbors, colleagues at work, friends or relatives who know the area. Don't be shy about asking them to recommend doctors, hairdressers, real estate agents and other service providers in the area. Also, remember your former physicians and service providers in your current city may be able to recommend their counterparts in your new city. They may not know anyone there, but these days you'd be surprised at how wide networks extend. Once you do relocate, your new co-workers and neighbors can be big helps as well in finding new physicians and service providers. All of these people can be instrumental in getting you settled. Also, Marcela always advises anyone relocating to take advantage of opportunities to socialize, so that you make new friends as well.

Amidst all relocation can bring in regards to relationship building, it also presents the challenge of figuring out where everything is physically. Before there were navigation systems, Marcela remembers driving as a big challenge with every move. Rather than getting frustrated with wrong turns, dead ends and seemingly-hidden freeway on-ramps, Marcela embraced the opportunity to learn her new city. She finds it energizing to figure out where her community is and where she's going to fit.

With all the change comes one constant for Marcela – her family. "You build very strong relationships with your family during these times of change. At end of the day, your family is your unit. It's the only thing that comes with you everywhere you go," she explained. Marcela's five children, three belonging to her and two to her husband, are all in their 20s now. They are all very independent and spread out across the country. She credits their independence and success to their ever-changing lifestyle as children. "Change," she stresses, "gives you energy and the power to do anything!"

Ask Mary

How do you know when it's time to leave a company?

This is a very challenging and very personal question that will differ for each individual. Mara Aspinall, CEO of On-Q-ity and profiled in Chapter 8, brings an interesting perspective to this issue. Over time, Mara developed the belief that there should be executive term limits, so people in senior management wouldn't stay in jobs beyond five or seven or 10 years at the maximum. Mara believes you only reinvent yourself a few times in the same job in the same place. You need to bring in new energy. At each point when she left a company, it was only after she felt she had done all she could.

I would add to Mara's perspective that you should also regularly evaluate whether you will be able to achieve your personal and career goals at a company. If you have development and promotion opportunities at your current company, then you should stay there as long as you feel you are making progress. Once you no longer feel progress is possible for you at a company, you should begin to plot your next move by answering some very key questions:

- Do I have the credentials and skills I need to move up?
- Will getting more education help open more doors for me?
- Am I living in the right geographical location for the opportunities I seek? If not, is relocation an option for me?
- Do I have strong references who will validate and supplement my job search?
- Am I financially secure enough to leave a company without having another job?
- Have I discussed this with family members, mentors, or others who will give me unbiased advice?
- Do I have a strong enough network of colleagues and contacts to help identify opportunities?

Answering these questions will help point you in

the right direction for your next move. But before you do any of these things, examine yourself, your emotions, your motivation and your energy level to see why you would want to make a move. Often I have found that sometimes a woman is just burned out and overwhelmed. It may not be a problem with your job at all. It may just be that you need a good break or vacation to refresh and re-energize your body, mind and spirit. Making a significant change should not be a hasty decision. It is one that requires a lot of thought and preparation.

Once you reach a definite decision to move on, you cannot look back. You must embrace the opportunity for change and look forward with great expectation and excitement to your new future and re-invention.

Chapter Highlights

- We are living in a time of constant change. Thanks to advances in technology, the way we communicate personally and professionally has changed much in the last decade. We are living in a global

community now with information at our fingertips. Colleagues around the world are a text message away, and we can do business like never before.

- The future is moving so rapidly, more and more
  will depend on your competencies and what you
  know. If you're struggling to stay ahead of the
  game now, it won't get any easier tomorrow. Tomorrow will bring even more technological advances, more things to know and more new concepts to merge, leading to what can easily become
  sensory overload.

- Embracing change rather than resisting it can
  make all the difference to your future success.

- One thing is for sure: If you don't learn how to
  grow with change, you're destined for fits and
  starts, delays and possibly denied dreams.

- It is more important than ever to develop as broad
  a range of expertise as possible, so be prepared to
  be a lifelong learner.

- In this world of globalization, there are better jobs,
  but none or few for the uneducated. In the future,

everything will depend not just on who you know, but on who and what you know.

- Remember that to change means to grow, to arise from what you once were and become what you always hoped or intended to be. It can energize and motivate you in unexpected ways.

- Through all the change you face, both personally and professionally, there is always one constant – your family

Chapter Six
Feed Your Mind – Learning for Life
"An investment in knowledge pays the best interest."
-Benjamin Franklin

"The jungle is dark, but full of opportunities," my 10th grade English teacher, Mr. Jackson, quoted. "An extra credit to the first person to tell me what it means," he continued. My hand shot up. "The world is hard, but full of opportunities," I ventured. He was quiet for a moment – probably shocked that anyone was that alert on a hot sleepy afternoon in the last class of the day - and then, with a satisfied nod, responded, "That's correct."

Although this occurred far too many years ago for me to care to mention now, I have never forgotten the phrase or the implications for women aspiring to become leaders, women with entrepreneurial affinities or women who just want to keep advancing. Women of power, progress and priorities must also be women of life-long learning.

Planning for your future corresponds to empowerment. There is no surrogate for planning ahead. And
it does pay off. All of the women interviewed for this
book acknowledged that charting a path and taking
definite steps towards achieving dreams and desired
wealth are a surer hope that leads to longer-lasting
gains than luck and the chance of beating the exorbitantly low odds you can bet on a lack of preparation.
Lifelong learners do not take a fatalistic attitude towards their lot in life. A proactive mindset is a must! I
made a choice that I would be the last poor person in
my family. That's why I got an education.

Halfway through my eight-year career at Kaiser
Permanente, the company went through a re-engineering process. The corporate structure was being
totally reorganized into areas to be led by an area manager. Job descriptions were rewritten with the goal of
becoming more challenging and strategic. Everyone
in any level of management had to reapply for his or
her job – in your current area or any other area – in
dreaded panel interviews.

In an interesting twist of fate, I was not hired for my current position. The new description for that position had been ramped up to include more facilities, and a new area manager was brought in from out of state. He opted to bring in someone from out of state for my role, someone he had worked with previously. Before I could commiserate on this turn of events, I got a call from my current boss to let me know that, although I did not get an area position, I had been selected for an interim regional position. That position was actually a promotion! Apparently, I received good ratings on the interviews I did – especially from the physicians.

In this interim role, I would report to the Senior Vice President of the Northern California Region who was also in charge of the overall re-engineering program. Both he and the CEO of the region were great mentors for me during this time. They both personally took the time to meet with me, coach me and help steer my development.

My development during this time centered on two things. While people on the interview panels loved my ideas, energy and dedication to the company, I did not do a good job of discussing the strategic approach for my role. My responses were very tactical. Secondly, the SVP and the CEO both advised me, in separate conversations, that I needed to go to graduate school and get a master's degree in either healthcare administration or public health.

Since my undergraduate degree was in communications, the lack of formal healthcare training was an impediment to my progress. It hampered my ability to facilitate strategic planning and thinking. While this was not the counsel I expected to hear, I made the decision to act upon their advice. It does not make sense to me to take your time and a busy executive's time for mentoring, if you are not going to follow the advice you receive. This does not mean that you will always agree or reach the same conclusions, but you owe it to yourself and to them to at least consider what you are being told. My SVP, Bernard Tyson and CEO, David Pockell, went so far as to contact graduate programs and write letters of reference for me. As I've already mentioned, I chose the health administration program at the University of Southern California in Sacramento.

In the vein of life long learning, I have to share one notable experience during this time. As you can imagine, I was indignant at the comments about my not being strategic enough and did not believe it was the case. Once I settled into the interim position, my new boss called me into his office and informed me that each regional department head had to write a strategic plan for his or her function for the entire region. This plan would then be implemented by the area functions. He gave me a two-week deadline for the first draft.

Okay, this is interesting. I had actually never written a strategic plan prior to this. But, I figured, how hard could it be? Right? On the due date, I met with him and presented the draft plan. He is a very affable guy, with a deep throaty chuckle. He read my plan, and then he gave me one of those deep chuckles before pushing it back across the desk saying, "No, this isn't quite it." I was mildly embarrassed. He gave me some feedback and suggested information to find and include and gave me two more weeks to bring the next draft.

I did all of the research, revised the plan and met with him two weeks later. He repeated the same pattern: read it, three chuckles and back across the table, two more weeks. I was mortified. I worked even harder, did more research, reached out to colleagues in similar roles in other regions of the company, contacted Boston College regarding its work in the field and fleshed out the plan some more. Two weeks later, I met with him to present the draft. This has to be it, because the deadline for all of the drafts was the coming week. He read it, still gave me the chuckle, but at least this time, he said I was getting close. He gave me a few more instructions and told me to come back in a week. I asked about the deadline and was told he would allow me an extension. I was beyond mortified, but also vaguely pleased that he didn't just take it and give it to the consulting group to finish as was happening with some of the groups.

A week later I was back with the next draft. This one, he proudly announced, was approved! I will tell you one thing. I never again got riled when I thought about the feedback that I was not strategic enough! It was not just something that is said when someone doesn't want to hire you.

That was one of the most memorable mentoring experiences in my career to date. It did more for my confidence and commitment to lifelong learning than anything up to that point. It was such a sense of accomplishment to see my plan rolled out for the entire Northern California region over the next couple of years. When I interviewed for higher promotions at subsequent organizations, I know that my ability to articulate an approach to strategic planning and possible strategic focus areas played a major role in my being selected for the positions. My former boss, Bernard Tyson is now a member of the C-Suite at Kaiser and is still a role model of mine. He has been a reference for me at the last three companies where I have worked.

The 2005 study on Experiences That Develop The Ability To Think Strategically, which I referenced in the introduction notes that the ability to think strategically is widely recognized as a key leadership requirement. Alarmingly, the study's findings suggest that an imbalance exists between male and female work experiences that develop strategic thinking ability. To bridge this imbalance, recommendations for female managers include specifically seeking out non-relational work experiences identified in the study, such as responsibility for major projects, handling threats to the business and participation in strategic planning and benchmarking processes. These were the areas where women were most lacking.

In my experience, not only did taking advantage of my Kaiser Permanente interim assignment as well as participating in the strategic planning process increase my confidence, it also gave me the solid leadership preparation recommended in the study.

Seek and Ye Shall Find Learning –In Every Experience

Lifelong learners do something every day to move toward achieving their vision – even if it is just reading a book or having a conversation with someone about it. The point is, we are always looking for and finding ways to stay engaged. We read industry journals, which catalog the latest developments in our fields. We attend professional development courses, which give us the confidence and knowledge needed to apply for that management position. We join professional organizations which give us access to speakers and mentors who can help us by sharing their journey. We apply for graduate school, even when it's not practical or easy. We listen to the constructive criticism of our superiors, because their advice can lead to our success. And through it all, we learn from our mistakes, so we can do better next time.

A lifelong learner does not hide the fact that she lacks knowledge in a certain area. She is keen enough to know that she doesn't know, and she also realizes it isn't knowing that always makes a difference. It is your motivation to do something to fix your lack of knowledge. A lifelong learner does not accept excuses or failures, but instead, goes out and seeks the knowledge needed to win, to succeed. Being a lifelong learner means possessing some humility. None of us knows it all. Those who boast they do often know the least. Those we revere for their expertise in a certain area or breadth of knowledge in a certain subject worked hard to achieve those standings. It was not handed to them. It was only attained after years of careful study and can only be maintained by many years more.

Power Up!
Dr. Beverly Tatum
President, Spelman University

My main source of inspiration for this chapter is Dr. Beverly Tatum, president of Spelman University in Atlanta, Ga. During my conversations with Dr. Tatum, some of which I shared with you in Chapter Two regarding her work/life choices dilemma, she talked with me about moments that have made a difference in her career. You have already read in Chapter Two her dilemma when the opportunity arose to lead the prestigious college. But what she shares here is how her commitment to lifelong learning opened this door for her.

Dr. Tatum always believed in investing in her own education. In her collegiate teaching career, she found herself at a couple of universities who did not have the funding to send her on professional development conferences around the country. During her time at Westfield State College in Westfield, Mass., where she served as an assistant and then associate professor of psychology, Dr. Tatum knew if she wanted to do anything costly (more than $400), she would have to pay for it herself. She made the decision to pay her own way to conferences. Colleagues would say, "I'm not going, if they won't pay for it," Dr. Tatum remembers. But she wanted the experience, the knowledge and the learning enough to make it worth it. Along the way she met a lot of people and learned a lot of valuable information.

When she was a young psychologist, no one knew who Beverly Tatum was, and there were people who were helpful to her despite that fact. She earned her bachelor's degree in psychology from Wesleyan University in Middleton, Conn., in 1975, and immediately went on to earn a master's degree in clinical psychology in 1976 at the University of Michigan, Ann Arbor. She completed her Ph.D. dissertation in clinical psychology also at the University of Michigan in

1984. She served as a dissertation fellow at the Center for Black Studies at the University of California, Santa Barbara from 1980-81, and through her studies, she became familiar with the work of Harriet McAdoo, a big name in research she had done on black, middle-class families.

During that time and later, Dr. Tatum would go to McAdoo's conferences to hear her talk about her latest research, and she would take the chance to tell her what she was working on. They were doing similar research. Dr. Tatum would position herself strategically at a conference to ensure a chance to speak with McAdoo. She would try to sit in the front, so when the lecture was over, she would be first to go up and introduce herself. Dr. Tatum would go up and ask questions of McAdoo, always with a copy of her own paper in her hand. "I would say, 'I'm working on something related,' and I would give her a copy of my paper," Dr. Tatum recalled.

She gave out her work, papers with her research, to people whose own work she admired and emulated. She still doesn't know if these other scholars she admired read them or not. But early on she was thinking strategically. Dr. Tatum knew when it was time to apply for tenure, one thing that would be asked was the names of people familiar with her work, people who could tell if she was any good. There was a need for external evaluators.

After teaching for six years and six years of attending conferences and handing out papers to famous people in her field of study, Dr. Tatum hoped her diligence had paid off. She hoped when these people got the call, they would at least know who she was. Being strategic is very empowering, Dr. Tatum says. Thinking about what you are going to need and positioning yourself, so you can meet those people who can give it to you is smart and, in this case, ultimately rewarding. If Dr. Tatum had said to herself as some colleagues did, 'the school is not going to pay me to go so I'm not going,' she would not be in the position she is in today.

Because of Dr. Tatum's perseverance, she moved on to a more prestigious position at Mount Holyoke College in South Hadley, Massachusetts, where she served as associate professor of psychology from 1989 to 1996. She eventually served as Dean of the college and Vice President of Student Affairs from 1998-2002 and then as Acting President in 2002 at Mount Holyoke.

Deciding to pay her own way to conferences led Dr. Tatum to valuable learning experiences she otherwise would not have had. They also started her on the path to success running a college. But, before that eventuality, she credits taking a chance on an internship for even steering her in the direction of clinical psychology in the first place.

Dr. Tatum knew some graduate schools preferred students with practical work experience. She knew business schools were more interested in students with some work experience as opposed to students right out of undergraduate school as well. She applied to clinical psychology master's programs right out of undergraduate school, but she knew her maturity level coming out of undergraduate school was important. She also knew she could possibly work as a research assistant or gain some experience in mental health work in an agency with her BA in psychology.

Options for internships and other positions vary from field to field. She knew even undergrads would gain experience through summer or school-year internships. The chance would help her gain clarity about her profession and whether it was a good idea to pursue it further.

Dr. Tatum heard a doctor from McLean Hospital, the largest psychiatric facility of Harvard Medical School, speak, and she wrote to him. She asked if she could serve as an intern, told him when she was available and what she wanted to do. She also said she would do it with no compensation. They worked it out, and she did an internship at the research hospital, working with children with mental illness.

This was the beginning of Dr. Tatum's taking hold of her opportunities and making the most of them, something she would continue to her whole career. There were two parts, she says, to this process: first, taking initiative and, second, seeking out opportunity to help you clarify your goals. "Sometimes, after the experience, you learn you don't want to do something. This can be very valuable as well, and it's better to learn it sooner rather than later," she said.

Learn How to Increase Your Value on the Job

I must take a moment here to point out what is obvious to most people – money is very empowering! In researching this book, I spoke to the Chairman of the Board and the CEO of the Women's Initiative who are both profiled in previous chapters. Women who use the services are dis-empowered by many external factors including racism, abuse, poverty and spouses or companions who are not supportive. They have reached out to the Women's Initiative in hopes of re-claiming some of their power. For many of them, this power will begin to return in the form of money, which will give them, again, the capability of taking care of themselves and their families. Giving these women the ability to pay rent on a home, buy groceries for the month and provide new shoes and clothing for their children creates a sense of pride and accomplishment that little else can.

Though, hopefully, most of you reading this will not need the services of the Women's Initiative, you may still feel powerless to change the course you are currently on. When you are feeling like this, it is important to remember that you are in charge, nothing lasts forever, change is coming and opportunities are all around you. You just have to open your eyes to possibilities, and let your desire for true empowerment propel you through the jungle of opportunities awaiting you!

It is important to recognize that not every place can contain every person. For some of us, it may be the stimulation of academic institutions that enables us to achieve our maximum potential. For others it may be the vast opportunities to give of oneself afforded by the church or other community organizations that can contain the fulfillment of our dreams and passions. It is interesting to note how some corporations have learned to create this "environment without walls" that stimulates instead of stifles innovation. These are the companies you regularly see appearing on the various lists of Best Places to Work in publications such as Fortune, Working Women or Essence magazines.

I was fortunate to oversee Genentech's submission of its application to appear on the Fortune Best Places to Work list when it was named #1 and #2 in subsequent years. The interesting thing is no company can just declare itself a best place to work. Its employees have to give testament to that reality. In our submission, our team let the employees tell the story of why they loved working there. Certainly the stock options for all levels of employees and compensation packages played a major role, but that was never the primary reason given by anyone. It was the opportunity to work on projects that made a difference to society, like the life- saving and life- enhancing products discovered and developed by the Genentech. It was being in an academic environment every day, where if you put forth your best effort and kept learning so you could add more value, you would be recognized for that contribution. It was knowing your ideas would always be heard and evaluated with all of the competing priorities and given a clear rationale for why they were or were not implemented. It was also understanding that "not now" does not mean "never."

This ties back to not only knowing how to create and engage in strategic planning and implementation, but also to taking it upon yourself to understand the company's overall strategic plan – not just your department or your function. People who are most successful at any organization have taken it upon themselves to study, understand and commit to not only the company's overarching mission, but its strategy and road map for the next three-to-five years that will get them there.

These plans are usually revisited annually and updated every three to five years. If you want to add even more value, find a way to participate in your group's update of its part of the strategic plan, so you become more familiar with the growth drivers of your company. If you aspire to be a woman of power, ideally, as you move up in the organization, you will move into more roles that are accountable for helping drive the growth of the company in the coming years.

You should never force yourself to fit into a confined entity, because you don't feel educated or prepared enough to do anything else. Ignorance is a dangerous thing. What you don't know can hurt you bad. Not knowing is dangerous. If you don't know, life is going to come after you anyway. The more you know, the more effective you can be. It is not just a matter of getting a degree and thinking you are done. Life-long learning means you regularly take classes, talk to peers, read industry publications to stay abreast of the latest advances in your field, attend seminars and conferences and read books. It should be ongoing.

This is vital if you are seeking to enhance your value to an organization. To improve your performance, you have got to get the words off the page and into your spirit – into your psyche. Otherwise, the hunter will get taken by the game. (As you read in Chapter 4, I like action movies, so my analogies sometimes are a little skewed!)

Ask for Learning Opportunities

The earlier example of my interim assignment at Kaiser Permanente and having to write a strategic plan is one way I gained the experience needed to take me to the next level professionally, while adding value to my company. It was a more daunting experience than I anticipated, but also a more rewarding one. Since it initially was a struggle for me and I was in an interim assignment, I could have easily asked my boss to have the consultants draft the strategic plan. But I would have never achieved the satisfaction of knowing I could learn how to create it.

I could read every book ever written about strategic plans, but nothing could get those words off the page and into my psyche more than having to create a plan for an integral function of a multi-billion-dollar corporation with 30,000 employees.

I would challenge you to find ways to take on new challenges. You need to aggressively pursue opportunities to develop and advance your management skills via on- the-job learning experiences. The Journal of Healthcare Management article mentioned earlier in this book notes that the largest and most well-known study of relevant managerial work experiences identified job rotations, scope expansions, special projects or challenging assignments and leads in start ups or turnarounds as conducive to general managerial learning.

The payoff for accepting such assignments is two-fold. You will likely learn a new skill set, which can be invaluable to you personally and to your career. You also will add value to your company, gaining the confidence of those who can promote you to the next level.

Ask Mary

How do I create a learning environment for myself, so that I stay at the forefront of my profession and my industry?

In order to stay at the forefront of not only your profession, but also your industry, you have to take the same approach as those considered leaders in specific areas. Remember, almost anyone can proclaim herself a leader, but that does not make it so. True 'thought' leaders are those sought out for their valuable contributions in certain areas.

First and foremost, you will find those true thought leaders are well versed in their subject matter. This comes from years of study. You, too, will need to strive for knowledge. Creating a learning environment means you have an obligation to be a scholar – continually increasing your knowledge and understanding on a certain topic. It means you will need to carve out a meaningful part of each day acquiring knowledge about an area of expertise, so that you can engage in dialogue with colleagues, clients and staff.

You can begin to gain this knowledge by taking advantage of any and all materials and training programs available through your employer. If you don't already have one, work with your boss to create a development plan, and do your research ahead of time to identify programs, classes or opportunities to gain exposure to new ideas, programs or thought leaders in your areas of expertise or in your industry.

You should also subscribe to one or two of the leading publications in your field, so you learn about new research, trends and future challenges. Attend at least one conference or symposium in your area to not only hear key leaders in the field, but also to engage in the spontaneous conversations that will occur as you meet people at the event.

Secondly, you have to be willing to be an educator - embracing the opportunity to share your thoughts and informed opinions with others. This is the only way you can test your ideas and solutions and make sure it is advancing knowledge in your area. Doing your research and keeping up to date on a regular basis will assure that you are not making off-the-cuff remarks, but rather thoughtful, educated insights.

Finally, as you grow more knowledgeable and have a definite process for continuous learning, start taking your leadership position. You will need to effectively and clearly articulate your learning and ideas. Get your feet wet by holding regular meetings with your team or peers to discuss issues and trends. Consider sponsoring a brown bag lunch session at your job on the latest topics or trends. Invite guest speakers. If you feel comfortable, moderate a panel or sign on as a panel member at a forum or symposium.

Be sure to remain current. Work the plan and gauge your progress. Do not fall prey to the pitfalls of many leaders who care more about getting their thoughts out rather than getting public opinion in. Find out the impact your profession or industry is having on society, and continuously brainstorm and track ways to improve the impact for everyone's benefit.

Chapter Highlights

Women of power, progress and priorities must also be women of lifelong learning.

- Never let your ego get in the way of pursuing knowledge. We don't know it all, and the most successful professionals among us realize this, admit it freely and do all they can all the time to rectify this truth.
- Lifelong learners do not take a fatalistic attitude towards their lot in life. Instead, they take action by educating themselves.
- Lifelong learners do something every day to move towards achieving their vision – even if it is just reading a book or having a conversation with someone about it. The point is they are always looking for and finding ways to stay engaged.
- Attending conferences, reading industry journals, listening to advice from superiors and taking on new challenges at work are just a few things life-

long learners can do to allow for more opportunities to learn new skill sets and keep up-to-date with trends and technology.

- Creating a learning environment means you have an obligation to be a scholar – continually increasing your knowledge and understanding on a certain topic. It means you will need to carve out a meaningful part of each day acquiring knowledge about an area of expertise, so that you can engage in dialogue with colleagues, clients and staff.

- Planning for your future corresponds to empowerment. The successful women interviewed for this book all agree that charting a path and taking definite steps toward achieving dreams and desired wealth lead to longer-lasting gains than do luck and the chance of beating the exorbitantly low odds you can bet on a lack of preparation.

- Being a lifelong learner is imperative to an entrepreneur's success. Fully operating as an empowered entrepreneur or executive requires a new level of mastery of the dynamics of persuasion and influence. This requires constantly honing and perfecting those skills and staying abreast of the latest advances in your field or business, so you can conduct meaningful conversations that demonstrate the value of doing business with you.

Good Reference Books/Websites/Magazines for the Life-long Learner

Below is a list of books I have found particularly helpful and are a part of my personal library. Most are available in your local library as well.

- NOW WHAT? 90 Days to a New Life Direction, By Laura Berman Fortgang
- Made to Stick, By Chip and Dan Heath
- Crucial Conversations, by Patterson, Grenny, McMillan, Switzler
- The 7 Habits of Highly Effective People, by Stephen R. Covey
- It's Showtime! Butterfield Speaks on the Power of Persuasion, by Richard Butterfield
- Daily Reflections for Highly Effective People, by Stephen R. Covey

- Prayers that Avail Much, Germaine Copeland
- Getting to Yes: Negotiating Agreement Without Giving In, by Roger Fisher
- Harvard Business Essentials Guide to Negotiation, by Harvard Business School
- Leading Change, by John P. Kotter
- What Got You Here Won't Get You There, by Marshall Goldsmith
- Strategy is Destiny, by Robert A. Burgelman

Websites:
- TheMissingMentor.com
- KnowledgePassion.com, a website created by Dr. James (Milo) Milojkovich
- Butterfieldspeaks.com, a website created by Richard Butterfield, communications coach

Business Publications

You should subscribe to at least one or two business magazines to help supplement your mentoring needs. I prefer Fortune magazine due to its regular profile of women and men in leadership and regular features seeking advice from various executives on current issues. Harvard Business Review is another one that features valuable case studies to help you in your quest for lifelong learning.

Of course there are many more general business magazines, but remember you need to do additional reading and research that is specific to your profession. It does you no good to subscribe to numerous publications and never find the time to read them. Try to set realistic expectations for yourself so you do not get overwhelmed and forsake all extracurricular reading.

Of course I do make time to occasionally read a women's magazine or fashion magazine, so I stay current on the latest hairstyles and dress. I also find them great motivation for weight control as well! Most importantly, they help me relax (usually while getting a needed spa treatment of some sort) and give my mind a break from the rigors of job and career focus. Remember, you need to take advantage of resources that help you take care of your mind, body and spirit.

Learning Dialogues

The list above will help you get started, but, by all means, add your own resources to this list and share it with others. Use the list as an opportunity to build friendships and create "learning dialogues" with colleagues, friends and neighbors. You can do these informally and begin to build your network of advisors as mentioned by Kim Thiboldeaux in Chapter 3 or mini-mentors described by Mara Aspinall in Chapter 8. Or, you can join regular Learning Dialogues chats online at TheMissingMentor.com.

Chapter Seven
Become a Power Jumper – Orchestrating Transitions
"The important thing is this: To be able at any moment to sacrifice what we are for what we could become."
-Charles Dubois

Resurrection Phenomes

Even without the assistance of a mentor, I have always been forward looking enough to periodically evaluate my progress, my current situation and where I see myself headed for the future. It is imperative that you step back, look at where you are, but also look at the horizon to see what is approaching in the future, where job and market trends are headed in your industry – or even what are some of the hot new industries you might want to try.

For example, when I was in college at the University of Louisiana and in my early career in television I was not happy with my pay, even though I was successful in landing my first on-camera television job while still in college,. As I did my research and talked to others in the field, I soon understood that I was not going to make any significant money unless I landed an on-camera position in a major market. I also came to understand that, as soon as my first wrinkle appeared, I would be out the door or out of the chair, so to speak. Added to this was the fact that I would have to start in smaller markets in towns where I had no desire to live in order to work up to major markets like New York, Chicago or Los Angeles.

After graduation I returned home to Chicago and then moved on to work in the advertising arena and landed a job at J. Walter Thompson advertising. But the salary still wasn't to my liking, and the work was not as stimulating as I had anticipated. Again, I was pretty low in the organization, and it was going to take me a while to move up to those higher floors where the action was. One of my bosses explained it to me. I was working in what is called the glamour industry – broadcasting, advertising and journalism. It is perceived as glamorous by others, and if you decide to put up a fuss about your salary or position, there is always some eager new face willing to take your place at whatever salary they are offered.

So I moved my focus to behind the camera and started producing and creating programs and fared a little better. It was while I was producing a television program for Lesher Communications Newspaper Group that I became interested in healthcare. The publisher of the paper and his wife became interested in adult literacy as a social responsibility initiative. Obviously, in the newspaper industry, you are concerned about people (especially adults) not being able to read. So, we created a partnership with the county library association and a local television station to produce public affairs television program called The Informed Viewer, that provided helpful information to viewers. The programs aired on the local station and were then made available in county libraries for checking out or viewing in the library.

I was asked by the publisher, Dean Lesher, to produce the programs. His wife, Margaret, was the host. Immediately, I became immersed in not just the glamour of television, but the opportunity to help others improve and enhance their lives by the information we provided, especially with the health-related topics. While Margaret's idea of health topics mostly centered on plastic surgery, I was able to branch out into more topics from there. One program focused on the healthcare dangers faced by adults who cannot read. I remembered hearing a story about a mother who gave her infant daughter eye drops orally – not just once, but for a period of days - because she could not read and was too embarrassed to tell the doctor or nurses or pharmacist.

It was then that I decided I wanted to make a transition in my career from broadcasting to working directly in healthcare. I eventually landed a job in Public Affairs at Kaiser Permanente. Because I did not have any health care experience, I had to accept an entry-level, part time position, but it got my foot in the door and, within six months, I was working full time. My career progressed nicely, and I was promoted every two years or so during my eight years at Kaiser.

As you read in previous chapters, my mentors eventually recommended I attend graduate school, and I enrolled at USC. One thing troubled me, however. In the back of my mind, I kept thinking Kaiser is a non-profit entity and as such, at the time raises were limited to approximately 2 percent every year. I questioned the overall financial benefit to my family of making such a commitment for such a costly graduate program. Therefore, I started my re-evaluation process during graduate school to see if I was headed in the right direction for the future.

The biotechnology industry was just starting to accelerate during that time, and we spent quite a bit of time in the healthcare finance and marketing courses studying new companies, including pharmaceutical, managed care and biotechnology companies. I also met classmates in the program who were working in all of the different health care industries, and I was able to get more information from them about the various opportunities including healthcare management consulting. I was interested in both management consulting and the drug industry. On the drug industry side, I specifically wanted to move into biotechnology. As I shared in Chapter One, I landed a residency in the management consulting arm of Kaiser as an entry-level analyst and worked there for a year. However, after the 10th or 20th cost-effectiveness analysis, I knew this was not the career path for me. After all, I did select my undergraduate major based on the least amount of math classes required! (It wasn't that I couldn't do it, I just plainly did not like it.) In hindsight, I was very fortunate to have this opportunity to increase my financial capabilities during the residency. I gained valuable financial planning experience that helped me advance to the more senior levels I have since achieved in my career.

Chapter Three on building networks details how one of my classmates connected me with an executive search firm to land my first director position at Bayer's newly created Global Biotechnology unit in Berkeley, California. Getting that position reinforced to me the approaches I discussed in Chapter Four about dreaming, planning, meditating on your future and where you want to go as opposed to taking a que sera sera, whatever will be will be, attitude to your career.

Pay Attention to the Writing on the Wall

When I began to see the level of funding for biotechnology decrease at Bayer, I started reading the handwriting on the wall and realized that if I was going to stay in biotechnology, I needed to move to a company where that was the main focus versus a large diverse organization like Bayer where biotechnology was just one of many business units. I had previously turned down two different calls from executive recruiters about interviewing for open positions at Genentech. As I mentioned in Chapter One, I really liked Bayer. I enjoyed the camaraderie and rapport amongst the entire leadership team. I appreciated the clear vision and strategy of the pharmaceutical and biotechnology divisions. I agreed with the value and focus placed on diversity and staff development. But, at Bayer, with such a small biotechnology pipeline, there would need to be a lot more funding to the business for it to become a major player in the industry. That funding did not appear to be forthcoming.

While attending the American Society of Clinical Oncologists medical conference in San Francisco,

I shared with one of my colleagues from the pharmaceutical division in Connecticut that I had declined at least two opportunities to interview for open positions at Genentech. She looked at me with incredulity. "What? You can't be serious?" she said.

Genentech was the first biotechnology company ever, and biotechnology is its core competency, so they don't have the same competition for resources from other divisions, she reminded me. "I know, I know," I responded. "I learned all about them in grad school, plus I have been tracking them as an industry leader ever since I came to Bayer. Trust me, if they call me again, I will definitely go in for an interview!"

Exactly two weeks later I got a call from yet another executive search firm about another open position at Genentech. It was a perfect fit for my credentials and experience. Although it was also a Director position and therefore a lateral move, I knew this was one of those open doors that I needed to go through. As the Director of Product Communications at Genentech, it was still a significant growth opportunity for me, because the company had a full pipeline with more than 20 potential therapies in its pipeline, plus several products on the market. I made the transition to Genentech. It turned out my instincts, as well as my timing, were good. Almost two months later to the day, Bayer had to pull a major product from the market and announced it was cutting back its biotechnology group as well as others. Most of my biotechnology colleagues ended up leaving the company, including my entire leadership team.

Be Proactive, not Reactive

To achieve the desired results orchestrating transitions has to be a proactive exercise – not a reactive one, where you wait until change hits and then try to get back on solid footing. This is also why prayer and meditation is so important. During that quiet time, you can gain the direction and leading you need to keep yourself ahead of the curve and in control of your life and your circumstances. Identify some warning signals for possible need to transition and do not ignore them if you see them. After the massive changes at Bayer, various colleagues from the company called me to ask me how I knew this was happening and why didn't I tell them. I explained that I didn't know. I just read the handwriting on the wall, having seen the reduction of resources, and through prayer and meditation about timing for my move, I felt in my spirit that it was the appropriate time to move on.

Sometimes this happens when you get a new boss or your access to promotions and new opportunities are not forthcoming.

Sometimes with a new boss, your ideas may not be valued and the whole idea of starting over to prove yourself is not appealing. First do some soul searching to make sure you are not intimidated or giving away your power.

This is a good example of the value of having an executive coach. Possibly you and your boss could benefit from someone to talk through your concerns, test your presentation of ideas and possibly even facilitate conversations to clarify personality and communication styles. Working out these differences and expectations are always critical in new working relationships.

As a new leader taking on a new team, a new leader integration session with a coach or organizational development facilitator is always a good first step to a successful transition for the team and the leader.

But the truth of the matter is there are just some times when it is obvious that your career aspirations are stalled and it is time to move on. When I felt it was time to make the move to a Vice President role, after taking an inventory of my current role, I knew that if the promotion was ever going to happen I would have to move to a new company. This is where orchestrating a transition successfully is key. This is not a time to burn bridges or enter silent rebellion or play the blame game. Blaming your boss or your company or yourself will not get you to where you want to be.

Instead take an inventory of your options and move forward. Maintain your energy and enthusiasm throughout the transition process.

Orchestrating transitions is also a great example of why you need to have a solid relationship with a few well connected executive recruiters. This will help you hit the reset button.

But the most important decision maker in this situation was the conversation with my children mentioned in Chapter 2. I had promised my children that their helping out at home and allowing me to complete graduate school would one day result in mommy being a vice president (as you will recall, this was planted in Mommy's head by Professor Myrtle at USC). My children never forgot it and cheerfully asked me on a regular basis if I had made it yet. I realized that if it were ever going to happen, I had to make some new choices. I decided then and there and began to say that not only was I going to be promoted to vice president, but eventually to senior vice president as well!

Working with an executive search firm I was able to secure that Vice President position at a fabulous Fortune 20 company. A little over a year later I secured a Senior Vice President position – all to my children's delight!

There are a lot of lessons in this example. The most important lesson is that you are not a victim. You are in control of your own destiny. Do not blame failure, delay or denial on someone else. In my opinion, you can give credit for your success to someone else if you'd like, but never blame for shortcomings, failures or misunderstandings. They, unfortunately, belong to you.

You will never get ahead if you keep stepping back. As I have mentioned previously, I like to win. Winning to me is making progress, advancing, moving forward.

Do not burn bridges. You could cuss out your boss or colleagues and quit, but, trust me, you will see them again. Join a company in peace and leave in peace. (More on this in Chapter 8).

Take a Chance on Your Dreams

Let me tell you about a question a woman once asked me during a question-and- answer session after one of my talks. She said, "I'm a 40-year-old woman who has worked over 25 years in my 'good government job,' and I have steadily climbed the career ladder, receiving numerous promotions. However, I am not experiencing the financial success I want and need to put my children through college. There are no higher positions for me here. But at my age, what else can I do?"

This question has come to me in varying forms, but the essence of the dilemma is, "Do I want to take any chances or not?" Of course every person's situation is different, and you have to assess your options according to your individual circumstances. That is what my head says about these situations. Now, disclaimer aside, my heart says, "If not now, when?"

My advice is to first search your heart to find out what it is that you really feel is your calling in life. What is it that you really want to do? What is causing this restlessness that is stirring in your heart after 25 years on the job? It has to be more than money, because if all you were really worried about was money, you would not dare dream of leaving the security of a job that is, in essence, guaranteed until you retire. The fact that someone is asking this question lets me know there is something inside of her saying, "I can contribute more. I have more to offer. I am wasting my talent. I am not being challenged. My best is yet to come." Of course, assuring our children's future is a strong motivator as well. But worrying and taking action are two different things.

She decided to make a change. She took the first step by preparing and applying for law school. To her amazement, not only was she accepted, but she received a full scholarship! She decided to take the early retirement available to her after 25 years of service in her government job and is now happily enrolled in law school. None of this would have happened had she continued to beat herself up about past choices. New choices are available to you every day. Create a plan for your future and take the first step towards it. Call the university and ask for an application. Take a prep course for the GRE or GMAT exam. Get a small business administration packet on how to start a new business.

You are seeing a theme here. To be a power jumper, you are going to have to do some research. Whether it is to create your strategic plan or find the niche that you are interested in, research is going to be essential to your success. Figure out ways to do research. You might begin by researching your area of interest online. Look at websites for companies who specialize in your area of interest. Read about individuals who have had success in that industry. Get your hands on industry journals that can inform you of current trends. Also, make sure that industry's future looks viable. It is important to make sure you transition to something that not only makes you happy, but that can continue to grow with you over the years.

Do not underestimate the value of creating a plan no matter how simple it might be. Once you have pinpointed a direction for your career, setting a timeline and sticking to it can make what is a now dream a concrete reality in your future. Check with others to see if it is a realistic timeline.

Find a few people you can trust and share your plans and possible actions. I must insert a comment here from the Bible that is very relevant whenever you are sharing a dream – "Do not cast your pearls before swine." It means do not share your valuable knowledge and dreams with people who will not appreciate them and will turn around and criticize you for it. They may even ridicule you or laugh in your face. In other words, as my kids would say - watch out for "haters." Hopefully, no one reading this book falls into that category. Many times people are not intentional haters. Its just that green monster, envy, rearing its ugly head. They merely feel jealous. When they see others moving on to pursue their dreams, they feel they are being left behind. Rather than using this as motivation to get going on their own back burner ideas, they ridicule or discourage others. Some people are just insensitive and rude, feeling, for their own reasons, that your decision is uninformed or ill-advised.

Face it, some people just may not have confidence in you. But that should not affect your confidence in yourself. There is a difference between needing someone's support and needing their vote of confidence or permission. The reality is that you may need the support of a parent, spouse, sibling or friend to achieve a goal. (However be prepared to find alternate support sources.) But you do not need anyone's permission to pursue your dreams. If you set yourself up mentally to need the permission or stamp of approval from someone you may really care about, you may be setting yourself up to be derailed.

When it's all said and done, only you have to walk this road to the resurrection of your dreams. Power jumpers have to learn how to jump over all types of obstacles – human, real and imagined. This includes dealing with setbacks like losing a job or having to accept a lower-level position in order to provide for your family as discussed in the Ask Mary section of this chapter.

Patience is another virtue for power jumpers that may be just as helpful as resilience. For example, I recently received this question from a young working mother:

"I have so many gifts and talents. But I don't feel like I am using them all at this job. I have been here one year and am being trained in a new skill as a medical assistant. I have three young kids to rear, but I don't want to do this the rest of my life."

In my response, I first reminded her that no one could do all things at one time. As mentioned by Dr. Marianne Legato in Chapter Two, women have to realize that the child-rearing stage is just one of many phases in our life. We have to deal with each phase of our life and not move prematurely before each phase has completed its cycle. In this instance, this young woman had not been on her job long enough to even know what all of her options or possibilities in her field would be. Since she didn't know what she wanted to do with the rest of her life, it might have been a better choice to take advantage of this time to raise her small children and enjoy the flexibility of a less demanding job.

Be a Flexible Power Jumper

Power jumpers have to be flexible. Several years ago, I heard Talk Show Host Beverly Smith speak at a luncheon in San Francisco. She shared how she cried when her television program was canceled. In her mind this cancellation signaled the end of her 27-year career in broadcasting. However, only a short time later, she was presented with the opportunity to become the only African-American woman to host a nationally syndicated program on American Urban Radio Networks. The Bev Smith Show has hosted featured guests including President Obama, former Vice President Al Gore and numerous entertainers. Beverly has received more than 300 awards and is recognized as one of the most important radio talk show hosts in America. She has been dubbed the 'Queen of Late Night Radio' and is a regular guest on Larry King Live. The cancellation of her previous show led Beverly to this amazing new phase of her career. We all need to be open to the opportunities awaiting us.

Flexibility is key to orchestrating any transition. I am a firm believer in the adage: "God does not close one door without opening another." But you have got to get up, and find and go through the door that is now opened to you. It could be the door to the most rewarding and stimulating phase of your life.

If you want to move into a new area; need to ease back into the marketplace after being out for a while; or if you are just not sure what you want to do, getting involved in a community effort of some sort can help create a skill set that will provide the desired transition. This could also be an opportunity for you to test a new skill set that you may be nervous about trying out a job with a new company. There is also great empowerment in giving back to your community through volunteering.

You can build skills around fundraising, leadership and organization, while working with people in so many different capacities. You may find opportunities to expand that you don't have in your current career. No matter how motivated you are, it is scary to get into something new if you don't yet have the skill set. By volunteering, you can try something new in an atmosphere where your help is appreciated and needed, and those around you tend to be happy to guide you along in your efforts.

Volunteering is also a great alternative if you are trying to build a resume. I have worked with colleagues who joined companies as volunteers in order to gain needed work experience after completion of a degree. This can be a mutually beneficial alternative. It gives employers an opportunity to receive free labor while evaluating a candidate's potential. It also gives the would-be employee an opportunity not only to gain experience, but to prove herself in a desired field.

In some cases, companies will allow you to intern for them. Though this option used to be reserved for soon-to-be or recent college graduates, some companies have expanded the option to include established or older workers as well. This is another way to get your foot in the door and try out a new career option to see if it is a good fit for you as you move forward.

You may find, after interning or volunteering, that a certain career track is not for you. It isn't what you expected, or you don't find it as rewarding as you thought you would. This is also valuable. You do not want to apply for positions that do not suit you. Experimenting with opportunities in this way gives you insight into the day-in-day-out rigors of a potential position or the overall demands of a certain company or industry. So, whether you determine you would like to go ahead and strengthen your skills in order to apply for a position or nix the idea altogether, you have made tremendous progress toward reaching your goal.

While you work to gain a broader skill set and true understanding of alternative career options, continue to share your goal with others who can support or advise you. This will help drive you forward as it creates support and eventually enables you to achieve your goal.

Even more importantly, share your resume with your mentor and others you trust to give you feedback and input. Make a special point of sharing it with people who regularly hire others, since they will be on top of the latest formats and approaches to sharing your experience. They will be able to share what they see in resumes that make them eliminate candidates from consideration and what they see that always interests them enough to bring the candidate in for an interview.

Also, ask those who are in a position to advise you, what else you can do to become a more desirable candidate for a certain industry or position. There may be an undergraduate or graduate course you can take at a local university to fill in gaps in your education or skill set. A leadership or technology seminar could add to your resume as well. Also, you may be advised to join a professional organization, where you can meet others in the industry and gain valuable insights regarding trends and future opportunities.

Becoming An Empowered Entrepreneur

This is even more important as you move through your life's journey and realize you want to try your hand at multiple opportunities - corporate, academic, professional, or entrepreneurial. Each step will involve new learning opportunities, resolve, confidence and ability to nurture and grow relationships among many other qualities.

For example, while company loyalty is an admirable quality and can certainly provide its fair share of opportunities, there is quite possibly no substitute for the sheer excitement (or terror) of launching out onto your own.

Indeed starting one's own business should be ranked at the top of the list for achieving empowerment. In her book, On Her Own Ground, Madame CJ Walker, the first known African American female millionaire said of her path to riches: "I started out as a field hand. Then I got promoted to a cook. Then I got promoted to wash woman. And then I promoted my-self." She parlayed an affinity for concocting hair care products, which she sold door-to-door in her spare time, into what became a multi-million dollar enter-prise shortly after the turn of the twentieth century.

Regardless of the venture, embarking on the journey to entrepreneurship requires setting and fol-lowing a path that is not always understood, popular or easy. It can truly be a dark jungle of unknown ob-stacles, pitfalls, surprises and success.

First and foremost, becoming an empowered en-trepreneur requires vision and innovation. You must move from knowing the diamonds are in the jungle to actually identifying, seeking and finding them. Iden-tifying true diamonds (innovation) versus, say, fire-flies is important, since you can have all of the vision and passion in the world, but if there is no need or desire for your commodity you will not achieve suc-cess or personal satisfaction. The homework and due diligence that must accompany the vision are essential empowerment tools. There can be no substitute for being a visionary and developing the ability to chart a path to achieve the vision. Empowered entrepreneurs understand that if you do not have a vision for your life, you will end up living someone else's vision.

Fully operating as an empowered entrepreneur or executive requires a new level of mastery of the dynamics of persuasion and influence. This requires constantly honing and perfecting those skills and staying abreast of the latest advances in your field or business, so you can conduct meaningful conversations that demonstrate the value of doing business with you.

Entrepreneurs are able to build support for the vision through their passion, personal presence and composition of compelling stories that open new possibilities to them, potential investors and employees. Once the target is in sight, you must be relentless and unstoppable in the pursuit of crystallizing the dream.

Speaking of investors, before you can convince someone else to back your business venture you must be willing to invest in it yourself. Aspiring entrepreneurs should practice tithing into their own business – especially when it is still in its formative stages. I like to use the biblical concept of tithing as a template. In biblical tithing, 10 percent of a church member's earnings are donated to sustain the church and, possibly, corresponding charitable organizations. This idea can be applied to funding a business venture as well. You tithe to your own organization – your business, faithfully every month. Create and donate to a "business venture fund" with a goal of 10 percent every deposit.

Of course, 10 percent may not be doable, so start wherever you can. However, before you talk yourself into a lower range, I recommend you look at your disposable income spending. When I personally began this practice to build funds to launch my own consulting business several years ago, I only needed to review my personal shopping spending to find the extra I needed. After a little over a year, I had enough saved to take the first step to entrepreneurship. Eunice Azzani shares in Chapter 8 how she used a severance package to start her family-run executive search business with her son and daughter-in-law. Julie Abrams and the Women's Initiative (profiled in Chapter 5) have dedicated major resources to helping aspiring entrepreneurs utilize their talents to realize their dreams.

Power Up!
Julie Abrams,
CEO, Women's Initiative

Remember the Women's Initiative for Self Employment we mentioned earlier? They provide high-potential, lower-income women the training, resources and on-going support to start and grow their business. The business management training, technical assistance, and financial services it provides — in English and Spanish — improve the quality of life for the women served, their families and communities.

Julie Abrams has been the CEO of the Women's Initiative for almost six years.

She finds not only empowerment, but motivation for her job from the mission of the organization and both the seriousness and success of the women they help.

Women who use WI's services are disempowered by many external factors, including racism, unsupportive spouses or domestic violence, poverty, not being paid what they are worth and lack of education. These life situations also reflect reasons why people are robbed of their power.

But Julie's philosophy is that each of us has to take responsibility for how we have allowed these situations to happen, and then we can turn them on their head regardless of how we got there. We can figure out how to move beyond it and re-focus.

WI's approach is to work with women to find out what triggers them to understand that they need to make a change or can make a change.

The program is 14 weeks in English and 18 weeks in Spanish. It is tied to the concept of micro financing, similar to the work in micro lending for which Muhammad Yunus just won a Nobel peace prize. WI loans are $200 to $25,000, with most averaging $2,000. After graduation, women can apply for the loan. Most of the women enrolled do not have a credit history, so they can't go through a normal bank to get loan.

"It's a journey," Julie says. "Fortunately, most of the women come to us at a point where they have crossed the threshold to have belief in themselves. Something happens to them before they walk in the door. They have mustered some courage or strength to say 'I can build this dream.' So they have a glimmer of hope when they walk through the door."

But Julie stresses that they are not fully empowered, because they are embarrassed when asked to say what their dream business is. For some reason, they do not want to say it out loud. One of the exercises in the classes is to have each woman draw a picture of where she wants to be, a picture of obstacles along the way, and a picture of how she is going to overcome them. And eventually, WI makes them say what their dream business is every day, so that by the time they graduate, they can say it with confidence and with their shoulders back.

Interestingly, mentoring is a natural outgrowth of the program. The women help each other, which in turn empowers and elevates them, because they are supporting others.

Women seeking a transition are more likely to seek training than men. "They have what it takes to launch a dream in them most of the time, and our methodology is about helping them discover what they already know. They just needed the confidence.

Many of the women have achieved success above and beyond what anybody may have imagined," Julie says.

Julie tells of one woman who wears a blue wig and has a great bakery business in Oakland with 17 employees. There is usually a long line of customers outside waiting to purchase her goods. She is an immigrant from Australia and was already an accomplished chef before relocating in the U.S. Another WI graduate was on public assistance for 16 years. She now has a massage therapy business with more than 50 contract employees. They provide on-the-spot massages in the workplace of major corporations.

According to Julie, many of these women have undergone a transformation. They came to WI after experiencing domestic violence or awful things and are now in a much better place. They are owning their own future and no longer behaving as victims. The most empowering thing for any woman is to not feel like a victim.

Julie has observed people who, when starting their own business, can almost physically kill themselves doing it. So WI helps them figure out what success looks like, what it takes to get there, and how they can stay safe and whole while getting there. The program includes an entire curriculum on this.

WI shares other criteria with its participants. The number-one indication of success for women in business is self-efficacy. In other words, confidence in knowing what you know. Many struggle with whether or not they are allowed to do it, often asking questions like how do I know whether I really belong in business. Making them understand they don't need anybody's permission to go into business is crucial.

Julie and her staff also connect events to bring influential women in business to speak to WI students. The average age for WI participants is 42, and a large majority are African American and Latino. WI graduates 350 women per year correlating into starting that many businesses per year as well. Overall, WI serves 2,000 women per year with mentoring and counseling. When they graduate and start a business, 35 percent of the women double their income within one year. WI also stays in touch to track their ongoing success. "We know they give back to their community. We know the income level they reach and that they have a tremendous impact, because they volunteer, contribute and hire others back into the community," Julie explains.

---

[i] McCall, Lombardo, and Morrison 1988

Power Up!
Nola E. Masterson, M.S.
Chairman of the Board
Repros Therapeutics, Inc.

An important concept when helping you understand transition has to do with levers or instruments of leverage, the concept of building toward something with every step you take or button you push. Nola Masterson understands transition well. In most cases, she chose to make professional transitions, because they allowed her to get closer to her ultimate goal: a "30-year plan" to gain enough experience to sit on corporate boards. There have also been cases where Nola was forced to transition because of unforeseen situations in her professional environment. She is no stranger to unwelcome transition in her personal life, either. But, with each change, planned or unplanned, Nola has always managed to evolve and ascend.

Nola's 33 years of experience in the life science industry began after she earned her master's degree in biological sciences from George Washington University. She went on to continue Ph.D. work at the University of Florida. She began her business career at Ames Company, a division of Bayer Healthcare Pharmaceuticals, and then spent eight years at Millipore Corporation in sales and sales management. Since 1982, she has been the chief executive officer of Science Futures Inc., an investment and advisory firm. Nola is currently managing member and general partner of Science Futures LLC, I and II, which are venture capital funds invested in life science funds and companies.

Her stellar work and reputation in the venture capital space helped make Nola the first biotechnology analyst on Wall Street, working with Drexel Burnham Lambert and Merrill Lynch. She also helped co-found Sequenom, Inc., a genetic analysis company located in

San Diego and Hamburg, Germany. In 2000 she was tapped to open the San Francisco office of Techno Venture Management (TVM), the largest venture capital fund in Germany.

Then, the unexpected happened: the events of 9/11. This caused TVM to backtrack from its goals in the U.S. as the country suddenly became a very unfriendly place for Europeans in terms of flying and security. The company made the decision to only have an East Coast office and closed its San Francisco office. While this changed Nola's course with the company, she was kept on as a consultant for five years, getting her closer to her ultimate goal. She used the unexpected transition to expand her horizons.

By 2004 Nola accepted a nomination to join Repros Therapeutics Inc.'s board of directors in Houston. For the next five years, she served on various committees including the audit, nominating and the compensation committees. In November of 2009, Repros announced Nola had been appointed Chair of the Board of Directors, effective immediately. She had reached a personal goal of hers in record time, thanks to effective transitioning throughout her career.

Today, she serves on a number of boards making decisions to advance companies and ideals she cares about. She is a member of the board of directors of Generex Biotechnology, Inc. (NasdaqCM: GNBT) located in Toronto, Canada. She also serves as chair of the Bay Bio Institute, a 501(c)3 part of BayBio, which promotes science education, workforce development and best practices as well as entrepreneurs in the bio-economy.

Though her professional goals were being met, Nola still felt restless. There remained within her a sense of needing to do something that would have more impact anything else she had done before in her life. This restlessness and need for change resonated from circumstances in her personal life as opposed to her professional one.

Although now happily married to her third husband, attorney Bruce Jennett, Nola carried hurt and pain over the death of her first two husbands. Both men died as a result of their service in the Vietnam war. Nola describes herself as twice wounded from the trauma of seeing them both emotionally go down in flames after the war. Her first husband was a West Point graduate who shut down emotionally after the war, ending the marriage. Her second husband and the father of her daughter did two tours of duty in Vietnam and drank himself to death upon returning home. According to Nola, the post-Vietnam trauma was worse than Vietnam for the families of veterans. Somehow, she knew she had to do something to make herself right with Vietnam.

Toward that end, Nola felt compelled to participate in a 2008 fact-finding mission with 15 women in the high tech industry. Their goal was to find out how Vietnam is working now. The group met with men and women to assess Vietnam's economy, schools, thoughts regarding ex-patriots, and goals of the ministers of trade and finance. Nola and the team got excited about Vietnam's growth and direction as a nation. She recalls the young people in the Vietnam banking industry being very anxious to meet Bill Porter, founder of Etrade, and wanting to model someone that successful.

Nola wanted to support the young professionals who reminded her of herself when she went to Wall Street in the early 80s to support biotech. Taking the trip to Vietnam gave Nola the perspective she needed to take what she considers one of the most significant steps in her career to this point.

Nola created an opportunity to help by putting together a fund consisting of a blue chip list of 15 Vietnamese publicly traded companies that allowed foreigners to buy in. The fund supports country infrastructure and helps build a middle class in Vietnam. Nola continues to build the back office for her fund and is looking for people with experience developing fund management documents. She is training a Vietnamese Stanford University student in this role as well.

Instead of allowing transition points in her life to derail her, Nola has used those events as levers to usher her to the next level. With the board seats and having started the fund in Vietnam, Nola now has the sense that she continues to help create public companies and a public market worth supporting.

Ask Mary

A couple of years ago, I was downsized from my company where I was in a director position. I had to accept a position at another company at a manager level. I have been at the new company for two years, and I want to move back up to a director position, preferably here rather than moving to yet another company. How can I achieve this goal?

My first step would be to have a conversation with your boss to share your long-term goals for the job and for your career. You need to seek your boss' advice and find out if you have her support in eventual advancement even if that means moving on to another department.

Next you need to work with your boss to create a development plan that creates a clear path to your goals. This plan should include not only identification of possible future jobs and promotions, but also continuing education or leadership development programs or courses to continue enhancing your skill set. You should do your own research to find potential courses or programs and discuss them with your boss when doing development planning.

Third, even though there may not be any director positions currently available in your functional area, you should ask your boss if there are any opportunities for you to take on a project management role for an important initiative in the company. This will provide an opportunity for you to showcase your senior management expertise to others in the organization. My word of caution, however, is to make sure that your day-to-day responsibilities are not neglected. The goal is to achieve this jump without sabotaging your efforts by getting so excited with the new that you neglect your real job. If she can perform these three steps effectively, it is my opinion this power jumper will be well on her way to jumping back to her previous level and beyond.

Chapter Highlights

- When you are beginning to feel the need for a job or career change, it is imperative to step back and carefully assess where you are and where you may be headed if you stay in your current job or make a big move. Look at the horizon to see what is approaching in the future. If you stay, where are job trends and market trends headed in your industry? If you decide to move on, what are some hot new industries that you might want to try?

- Be tuned in to what is going on in your current industry or company. Are there cutbacks in your department? Is the industry losing money around the country? Is your company unwilling to invest in your division? Do not ignore these signs and blindly trust in the company line. If you have identified some warning signals for a possible need to transition, take heed of them. If the future looks bleak, it may be time to move on.

- To achieve the desired results, orchestrating transitions has to be a proactive exercise – not a reactive one where you wait until change hits and then try to get back on solid footing. This is also why prayer and meditation is so important. During that quiet time you can gain the direction you need to keep yourself ahead of the curve and in control of your life and your circumstances.

- The most important lesson here is that you are not a victim. You are in control of your own destiny. Do not blame failure, delay or denial on someone else. You can credit your successes to others, but not your failures. They belong to you.

- If your job is secure, but you find yourself restless, ask yourself why. What is it you really feel called to do in your life. What is it that you really want? And, remember, in most cases, it isn't money you are looking for. It is something closer to the heart than that. Spend some time evaluating what this is.

- Ask yourself these questions: What are your talents? What could you contribute that you are not? What can you offer that no one else can? Are you being challenged? The answers you give can go a long way to getting you where you want to be professionally and personally.

• Flexibility is key to orchestrating any transition. Remember the adage: "God does not close one door without opening another." But you have got to get up, and find and go through the door that is now opened to you. It could be the door to the most rewarding and stimulating phase of your life.

• The path to your proper transition may not be direct. You may wind up volunteering, interning, taking classes, joining professional organizations, reworking your resume and, possibly, changing your intended course. As long as, in the end, the path leads you where you want to be, enjoy the journey and all you learn along the way.

Chapter Eight
On Track – Avoiding Derailment

"One of the most valuable lessons I learned … is that we all
have to learn from our mistakes, and we learn from those
mistakes a lot more than we learn from the things we
succeeded in doing."
-Gov. Ann Richards

If you have absorbed the information and advice in the previous chapters, you are well on your way to managing power, progress and priorities. However, even the hardest working woman, who has prioritized and planned out every step of her family life, career and future aspirations cannot make amends for what I call "fatal flaws." One of the major reasons I have been drawn to providing mentoring counsel and advice is because I have seen so many bright and talented people with promising futures end up derailing their potential because of missteps or character flaws.

A missteps or faux pas; an error in judgment or conduct; a bad or awkward step; or a step in the wrong direction – however you define it--, there are certainly pitfalls to watch out for that can derail your work, credibility and career.

Some of these flaws include, but are not limited to:

- Lack of social graces or business etiquette
- Inability to conduct oneself in a corporate environment
- Insecurity
- Too ambitious
- Intertwined personal life with workplace
- Burned bridges

The list can become quite long. In this chapter, I have described some de-railers and how to recognize and overcome them. I have also asked some of women profiled in this book to provide their insights on some things women should watch out for that can derail their best efforts.

1) Coming across as either too female or too male

During her career Catherine Arnold (profiled in Chapter One) has seen women try to overcompensate for being in a male-dominated environment by putting on a "tough guy" persona, complete with dropping swear words and assuming other "male" behavior to fit in with the men of the company. However, Catherine noted, these women are not fooling anyone –especially the men. Don't overcompensate by trying to have too much of a macho, bravado demeanor, she advises. You will fall flat and fail to fit in. Instead, you may look foolish and not be taken seriously.

But by the same token, if a woman is too female in a male environment, she will quickly get left out of powerful decision making, powerful positions and opportunities. Her progress will be hampered. To avoid this, women should not be overly accommodating or overly nice. Those behaviors may endear people to you personally, but professionally there is a big downside. This behavior may result in people over-delegating to you, misusing or under utilizing your skills. For example, many times in meetings women take on the role of hostess by doing things like offering the speaker a bottle of water or getting up to give the speaker coffee, while men sit firmly in their seats. If you are the only one doing that, you are eroding your power. One solution may be to ask a colleague closer to the speaker to please pass the water. Do not put yourself in the role of hostess and serving others.

Along those same lines, a woman's power can be usurped when she is overly emotional and/or sexual at work. According to Eunice Azzani, men don't want to see people crying or having various emotional displays or doing the "en garde" (as in a fencing match) thing. Over the course of her professional career, she has seen women make the major faux pas of trying to use sexuality to propel their careers. It doesn't work very well when you use that either to try to get attention or to move up the career ladder, she stressed. Going that route can totally damage your credibility and hinder your progress.

Women often want to be seen as one of the guys or part of the 'in' crowd. But, according to Eunice, women need to understand they will never fit into the guy club. Women really just need to be seen as who they are, while also understanding they do fit into the big picture.

2) Very wordy women quickly derail themselves.

When giving a speech, women tend to say 50 percent more than they need to with the notion if I give you more information, it will be more helpful to you, I'll appear smarter and my speech will be more complete. Women tend to lose people in delivery, because they say too much. Men are much more abbreviated when speaking and get to the point more quickly. Men challenge listeners to pay attention, to think beyond the words being said and to come to their own conclusions.

As a rule, I, and the other women profiled in this book, have always found it particularly helpful to practice any important presentation with members of my team. I also practice with other teams who may not be as familiar with the subject matter, to make sure I don't get bogged down into too much detail. I want to present just enough to make the key points and articulate my "asks" or decision points needed.

3) Fear is unequivocally the fastest derailer anyone can encounter.

A woman of power and progress cannot be afraid

of her people. She cannot make a decision based on who will believe her or who will be mad. Linked to fear is insecurity or feelings of inferiority. As I mentioned in previous chapters, some corporate cultures can "smell the blood," and once they do, they will go after it and root out anyone who is fearful. If you think about it, you can understand why. In every organization there is a lot of money on the line, a lot of people's jobs and livelihood are at stake, and if it were to allow fearful people to hinder decision-making and progress, the results could be disastrous.

If you struggle with fear, it is important that you get to the bottom of what is causing your fear and take steps to overcome it. If it's fear of making a mistake, then get data to help you make the right decisions. If you don't exactly know what to do in a particular situation, do some benchmarking of how other companies handled similar situations and customize a specific solution for your organization. And by all means, ask for help. Gather the opinions of others. This is where a mentor can be very valuable. But remember if you have or are planning to acquire a mentor, come to that person prepared with options, ideas, data and/ or benchmarking. You cannot just show up and expect them to help you solve a problem or find a solution without having done your homework. Help yourself as much as you can, so they can better help you.

4) You must "honor the point."

While I am not a hunter, I know pointers are dogs who help hunters flush out prey. While there may be multiple pointers accompanying a group of hunters, whenever any pointer sniffs out a prey, it stops in its tracks, gets quiet and points its whole body, head and nose, in the direction of the prey as if to say, "It's over here. This is where you need to go." Interestingly, once any pointer points at prey, all of the others stop and point in the same direction, no matter where they may be in proximity. It is called "honoring the point."

In other words, you need to respect the due order, the authority of the leader of the group, team or the company. Anytime this disrespect happens, the train is heading for a derailing. Remember, anything with two heads is a monster!

Being so ambitious that you will do anything to move up can cause you to violate the due order of a company or department. Aggressive ambition of this sort is easily recognized by others and leads to lack of trust - thereby hindering the very progress you may be seeking.

Eunice Azzani notes that women, especially, need to be cognizant of a culture that does not traditionally recognize women leaders. This is why it is imperative that women respect other female leaders. I have seen many women derail themselves, because they do not honor the point if the pointer is a woman. These same women do not have that problem if the leader is a man. I have had two unpleasant experiences in my career at two different companies where women on my team have not honored my point. In both cases, I later found out that each woman had set her sights on my job – unbeknownst to me. As this is negative behavior that only begets negativity, it was not long before both women ended up out of those organizations. To add insult to injury, after some time passed, both contacted me about being job references for them! (More on that in the bridge burning section!)

I used an offbeat analogy to illustrate this point recently when speaking to a group of graduate students. I heard the story from a friend who used to be the secretary of her church choir. She is a naturally observant person and shared how she noticed the difference in response between the men and women each week when the choir president would announce the color scheme for the coming Sunday. If the president said the color was gray tops and black bottoms this week, the men would listen intently, make a note or just nod their heads as in "got it" and say nothing. On the other hand, it never failed that amongst the women there would immediately be grumbling ("Gray! Why do we have to wear gray? I don't look good in gray.") My point was that in my almost 30 years of executive leadership and management, I can truly say I have only had problems with women not honoring my point – not men. At the end of the session, one male student raised his hand to say he was looking for a job, loved the company I worked for at the time, and he would happily wear his gray shirt (that he was actually wearing that day) any time I gave the word!

Whenever you refuse to follow or obey the due order, you need to make the appropriate adjustments to correct it. If you are the one causing discord in your office, you need to get over it or get another job. If you are a leader and have people on your team causing discord, you need to get rid of them. I have had two instances in my career where two of my informal mentors outright advised me to remove people not honoring my point. It was the most difficult advice I ever received from a mentor, but wisely (and appropriately) taken.

The whole concept of gunning for another person's job is a major part of this analogy. It is not a new concept in the corporate world for people to scheme to take someone else's job, but there is a way to let people know your goals and how you would like to progress in your career without conniving, scheming, or attacking another person's character or talents.

I will add, however, an observation made at a recent forum. There is less and less of this type of behavior going on among the 35 and under age group in the female work force. This group seems to have been born, raised and trained with the notion that they have to compete on their merits, skills, talents and intelligence. This is in contrast to many women in the 35 and older age group, who may have encountered more obstacles and hindrances, and due to this, have opted to make progress happen by less-straightforward methods. This can be considered a fatal flaw, because it can backfire at any time in your career and derail your credibility.

Also, beware of flatterers. Do not get caught up in flattery. It is sad to say, but there is no such thing as total trust in the workplace. Many times, the one who tries to get closest to you, is always smiling at you and is going out of his or her way to buddy up to you is the person you may need to watch out for the most. There is something to be said for keeping a certain amount of emotional distance between you and your staff, while still remaining supportive and engaged. Many of the women I profiled shared this same caution. Either find friends in the workplace who are peers or in other groups outside your own, or just make sure you have an active, vibrant personal life outside of work, so you are not depending on work colleagues to meet your social needs.

5) Not staying in your lane

Everybody is not an expert at everything. How hard can a particular thing be, you ask? Well, it can be really hard if you don't know how to do it. This also applies to spouting off stuff you don't know, because it is not in your area of expertise. You need to stick to what you know.

I once worked with a consultant who was a brilliant strategist, but I found out later she absolutely could not implement. She led stimulating strategic discussions about a new focus area for our group and created compelling presentations to sell it to me and other executive leadership. Once the initiative was approved, our natural thought was to hire her to implement the exciting strategy. She was not with the company a month before we started getting complaints across all levels of staff and stakeholders, and it became very obvious she had no idea how to implement the initiative.

Unfortunately, she was in total denial about her abilities and blamed lack of movement and coordination on others. She soon left the company. This was a person who did not understand her lane. She could have been much more effective staying in a consulting role, where she added tremendous value and could work with a variety of clients who typically had scores of implementers, but not as many strategic thinkers and planners.

6) Being a people pleaser or trying to make people happy

This can turn out to be a super fatal flaw for women, whether you are the one trying to make someone happy or if you are the one expecting your boss or company to make you happy.

In my first job as a department manager at a television station, I inherited one employee who was an exceptionally good writer, but had a job preparing daily program logs. Let's call her Ms. A. She complained every day about not being happy with her job and wanting to do more in the line of advertising and promotions. So, I had regular conversations with her about roles or projects on which I thought she would like to work. I handed her new opportunities, and I expected to see a smile and some pleasure at being able to expand her skill set. Instead, I only met more glum expressions each day.

In addition, I had regular encounters with different station personnel to whom she complained and who would advocate for her. They would tell me how she shared her unhappiness with them, and they would then ask if I could do something to allow her to do more of what she really desired to do. This even went as high as my boss, the general manager of the station. So I kept trying.

One day, the general manager called me into his office to ask that my department take on a new role in the company, handling promotions for the station, including writing copy, creating promos and writing scripts for community programs. It was quite obvious he was giving us this opportunity for Ms. A's sake. I remember thinking, "Wow, how nice of a company to do something like this for this person." Surely I thought Ms. A will be pleased with this opportunity.

I went in with excitement and told Ms. A about the opportunity. Instead of a thank you – or even a smile, she looked me in the eyes and, in a tone of total disdain, said, "Okay, but to be honest with you, I don't want to do that." I could not believe it. I was done! I raised my eyebrows and looked her back in the eyes and said, "Ms. A, people in our industry would kill for a job like this. I don't know what else to do for you. Your problem is you don't even know what you want yourself. You do not want to be happy, so you are never going to be satisfied." "Well then in that case," she responded in a huff, "I might as well just quit then, huh?" "Yes," I replied. "That might be the best thing for everyone involved." She immediately got up, packed her things, and left the company. Although I was extremely irritated with Ms. A's response, I was also increasingly concerned that I had to go tell the station manager that our plan to appease apparently backfired. Imagine my relief when I told him she quit and his response was "Good! We've been trying to please her for years and she was never satisfied."

I just need to add a caveat here. It is entirely possible that your position requires you to be a people pleaser. If you are in a support role as an administrative assistant, provide customer service for a company or have recently acquired an entry-level type position, there is an expectation that you will focus on pleasing the customer or the executives you support. It is important to make the distinction, I believe, because later in life, when you reach a supervisor or manager role, you need to understand that your tasks have changed fundamentally. You are no longer required to please everyone on your team, which is a good thing, because you rarely can. The task falls to them to find their own happiness with the company and with themselves.

7) Burning bridges

"You know where you've been, but you don't know where you're going." My foster mother gave me this sage critique when I started my first job. It was her way of telling me to treat everyone right and do the right thing, because further down the road, you don't know what might happen or whose help you may need. As mentioned previously, I have had the unfortunate situation of being asked to be a reference for people who had totally burned the bridge with me, and I was frankly flabbergasted that they had had the audacity to ask for a reference. My motto is "join a company in peace, and leave in peace." That applies to relationships and any other entities in which I am involved, like community groups, schools, churches and social organizations. I have met some parents or coaches in my children's sports programs who behaved poorly and then wanted to network. This rarely works out well. As a rule, be nice to everybody, and they are more likely to be nice to you. These are simple playground rules at work here.

If you do find yourself in a situation where you may have burned a bridge and you want to reconnect with the person, you have to start with acknowledging your missteps and offering an apology. See if they are willing to start over. The worst thing you can do is try to pick up where you left off and never even acknowledge the problem.

Finally, remember to "keep words soft and tender for tomorrow you may have to eat them."

8) Being a whiner or assuming the victim role.

Of course men can be whiners as much as women, but in my experience, I have come across far fewer male whiners than females. "Whining will kill you professionally," Eunice Azzani says. Whiners naturally take on a victim role and that exudes exactly the opposite of the position of power and confidence needed for the company to entrust you with more responsibility. A female colleague at Korn Ferry fell into the victim role, and Eunice tried to coach her out of it, explaining that male colleagues would not listen to her, and her opinions would not be valued, if that's the way she approached things.

Eunice never understood why this woman felt she could not do what she wanted to do because of someone else. If you hear yourself saying, "I couldn't do this, because someone wouldn't let me" be careful. You are assuming a victim role. Only you control what you can and cannot do. Do not whine away your power!

9) Not listening when people give you feedback.

Not allowing feedback to be absorbed will definitely derail you, because if you don't accept the feedback, there is no way you can make the necessary adjustments to correct a flaw or to get back into balance. I am a big fan of self-confidence and self-esteem, but no one is perfect – including you. Even if you are really good, you can get better. We should all seek an environment of helpful feedback.

Eunice shared some feedback with me which she's heard over the years regarding other women leaders. The comments include "too pushy," "doesn't listen well," "doesn't ask the right questions," "talks too much," "doesn't have the right experience." She observes men take feedback and adjust to it, because they want to do well in the political spectrum of a company. Women want to say, "If that's not right, I need to stand up, and let you know it's not right." But that can bring some problems. If you don't agree with feedback and want to draw attention to it, you are then pegged as too strident. Eunice says she has been called "too" everything and has still been very successful. Receiving negative feedback in itself is not a derailer - it's how you receive it and respond to it that can derail you or further you down the right track.

10) Getting derailed by responding inappropriately to major opposition; envy or jealousy; or attacks on your skill set and credibility.

Mara Aspinall faced major opposition throughout her career due to a desire to stay at the forefront in various industries and not get stale. She spent 14 years at Genzyme and learned how to keep going forward and remain successful in spite of opposition. At Genzyme, everyone was fine with her heading up a small division, but as soon as she was doing a merger and creating a larger division, people begin to say, "Wait a minute, you stay over there. Diagnostics is not as big. It 's a zero sum game. Why do you think diagnostics should be as big as a therapeutic business?" There was no interest in her division being as big as others.

Mara says the way to deal with this type of opposition is:

1) Be intellectually honest with yourself. Make sure you believe enough in what you do and you like the people you're working with enough to fight for it. Recognize that there will be times you are challenged enough with people you don't like. (Versus people you don't respect. If you don't respect them, you should not be there. Move on, and don't fight adversity). Since she had a good story and good passion, she knew she could turn both divisions around at Genzyme, make them profitable and add shareholder value. Mara notes that, if she didn't believe she could do it, she would have listened carefully to adversity and probably not taken the positions.

Know that you don't have to have all of the answers 100 percent of the time. Mara sees a lot of women say "I can't be absolutely sure I can hit the 25 percent growth figure."If you can get close to it, take the calculated risk that says you can do it. But don't do it if you think it's only 2 percent.

2) Be clear where you want to go next in your career. If taking on this challenge helps you to get there, then see it as just another battle against adversity.

3) Get your data. Understand that making an argument will be successful only to people who will believe you. But you are usually making an argument to people who will be more skeptical, and for those people, you need data, not just your passion and commitment. Use data in a proactive, positive way – not defensively. At both the law firm and drug company where she worked Mara got huge pushback for new programs and ideas. At her law firm, she sat down with data and said, "Show me where this is wrong." At Genzyme, she made the statement, "I can get this biz to profitability" and had to show them the path. Too few people are willing to do that and get angry and leave the company.

4) Mara especially sees too many women, when challenged take it too personally. The reality is sometimes it might be personal. But she has gone through life assuming it's not personal unless someone makes it really clear that it is. Many young women should not as-

sume it's personal on day one. And if it is most of the time you just need to move on and not let it affect your psyche. No one is liked by everybody.

One other experience was a catalyst, causing her to take risks in her career. On her first day of class at Harvard Business School, the professor wrote – drop dead. He then told the class these are the two most important words to remember. What he meant was drop dead money.

Early in your career, try to build the financial flexibility to be able to take the risk if you ever find yourself in a situation where you can't stand what you're doing. Many people work in stable roles, and though they might want to take on the risk of a new start up, they cannot live with the possibility of re-duced income in order to pursue their dream. They just don't have the flexibility. Think early enough to build up a financial nest egg to take a risk and if it doesn't work you can still eat. This financial reserve can be key to you being able to take a new oppor-tunity, to say "go for it," while others may not. Not everyone can do that financially.

Take risks and continue to grow using some of your same base skills. Know what your hub of skill sets is, since it doesn't change tremendously in life. Start with that hub and put spokes off of it. Occasionally a spoke creates its own hub, but you are still using major skills, communications and management. As a junior person, you don't always know what your hub is, but become comfortable testing some spokes out of your current skill set.

Power UP!

Mara Aspinall
President & CEO
On-Q-ity

Mara has had an unusual career. She describes it as a "collage career," meaning she has worked in multiple industries in mostly management positions. She attributes her collage approach to her desire to always be creating something new, which has been the one connecting piece in all she has done. That desire has led her, on more than one occasion, to leave flourishing positions to take on new challenges fraught with risks.

Mara graduated from Tufts University with undergraduate degrees in international relations, Chinese history and Chinese language. Mara attributes her creative mindset and capability to her liberal arts degree, which gave her a tremendous amount of broad knowledge and an expansive way of thinking.

Her career began at Bain and Company, where she provided advice and counsel to healthcare and information technology clients. She eventually enrolled in Harvard Business School and earned an MBA, becoming vice president of her class, while enjoying a growing understanding of the classical business dynamic.

Mara understands the desire women have to take advantage of all our interests. Even in high school, she was being creative, volunteering to serve as the staff photographer for New York's Mayor Koch during a summer internship, after the regular photographer broke his leg. Photography remains her personal passion, and her initiative in gaining the internship resulted in a chance to have her first photography exhibition in City Hall. Her subjects ranged from prison guards to librarians to student interns.

Mara returned to Bain after business school and became the first female partner, but after a few more years, she had enough of telling other people what to do and wanted to do it herself. Mara stepped into a totally new world and role at Hale & Dorr law firm in Boston. The role was innovative in a lot of ways, since Mara was not a lawyer. The CEO of the company believed lawyers do not know the business of running a law firm and should focus on their own expertise, so he brought in a business professional with a Harvard MBA to run the $250 million company. Mara handled external relationships and internal strategic analysis at the firm. She started with a shared secretary and ended up with a staff of 12 when she left.

Mara says she could have easily derailed herself the first day when she went to the partners' meeting and was introduced as a new senior staff member and no one applauded. She found out later that day that applauding new hires was a tradition at this premier firm, and she had been the first one to be introduced to no applause. She was in for a shock later that evening at a company reception when she went to shake hands with a partner. He said, "I will not shake your hand. I did not want you here, and I do not want any of your kind here." He then turned and walked away with Mara's hand still out there. Fast forward to the day she left the firm seven years later. This same partner came to her office and said, "It was a pleasure getting to know you, and thank you for your time here." "It was not quite 'I'm sorry,' Mara admitted. "But, I didn't need it [the apology] anymore."

Mara has no complaints about the seven years in between those two events, even though it was the only time in her life she had to put up her Harvard MBA diploma on her office wall. After she proved herself, they became more open minded and respectful. On her first anniversary at the firm, a senior partner came up and handed her $25. Ever professional, she responded, "Thank you, but what is this for?" To which he replied, "We had a pool that you wouldn't last for a year, so I felt it only fair you share in what I won."

Despite having no mentor during her time with Hale and Dorr, Mara became nationally recognized for marketing law firms, speaking around the country on her work. Her firm went from #6 in Boston in profitability to #1. During this same time, companies like Pepsi and General Electric began hiring Chief Marketing Officers, when in the past those functions at many companies were mainly held by administrative staff members who had been promoted into the role. Ninety percent of those positions were held by women, and even at consulting firms like Bain and McKinsey, there were no partners concentrating on marketing. Today it's more integrated gender-wise, with higher salaries. And it's become a well-valued function.

Since she did not have mentors, Mara had to be very diligent in assessing her situation on a regular basis. In looking over her career, she had gone from consulting and improving businesses to a company where she was not a principal and was not going to make it more successful through legal skills, which was the core of the firm. Her model was to make significant changes in one firm and use it to transition to another.

Even more importantly, Mara says this was the beginning of her belief that there should be executive term limits, so people don't stay in jobs beyond five, seven or 10 years at the max. Mara believes you only reinvent yourself a few times in the same job in the same place. You need to bring in new energy. At each point when she left a company, it was only after she felt she had done all she could.

After leaving the law firm, Mara received an offer from the biotechnology company, Genzyme, and within nine weeks of joining had put together a strategic plan for the smallest division of the company that was losing money and was not well respected internally. The CEO was so impressed that he asked her to become president of the division, even though she had only been there nine weeks. Mara had no illusions, however, knowing she was the second or third choice, but not allowing this to insult or derail her. She considered it a fabulous opportunity.

After heading the division for four years and grooming a successor, Mara again felt her job was done. She had done as much as the group was able to handle. She went to the CEO to announce her intention to move on, and he convinced her to stay another year, citing concerns that the successor was not quite ready. After a year, she was appointed to head the diagnostics division and then the genetics business. Her groups went from 50 to 300 people and then from 600 to 2,000 people. She did four acquisitions, including a major one which doubled the division size after buying a company out of bankruptcy resulting from fraud.

In the diagnostics arena, she bought a cancer diagnostics firm and worked at the forefront of personalized medicine, chairing a coalition, regularly speaking and recently authoring an article for Harvard Business Review on the challenges and opportunities around it. Mara's desire to create and work in the forefront still garners public contention. At one forum 10 years ago, a physician stood up during one of her speeches and walked out saying, "This is insulting. I personalize everything I do." Instead of letting these things derail her, Mara takes them as confirmation she is on the right track and still creating reality from ideas.

After 14 years at Genzyme, running three different businesses, she again hit a point where she questioned whether she had done all she could there. Since the company still wanted access to her expertise, she created a different approach, taking a sabbatical instead. She divided her time by working at Genzyme 25 percent of the time, while spending her remaining time working at Harvard Medical School. Many peers and colleagues thought it was crazy to make this move at the height of her career. But Mara felt she was stale and needed to renew herself. The business was at a new stage, and she felt she was not the best leader. The company had grown to the stage of focusing on improving operations and processes with more block and tackling for which she felt she was not the best person and would not be challenged. She found a successor and moved to her new arrangement.

Mara notes that she tried to find mentors during this time, but could find none other than her husband. Once her arrangement was announced, even senior people at Genzyme said, "Wow, how did you get the idea to do this." At an industry meeting with a group of CEOs, she announced her plans. One CEO pulled her aside and said, "I don't like this. It is an inappropriate risk and will get you off the leadership path. Do not mention this to anyone else on my team." Yet another said, "I'm stale. Talk me through how you found a successor, how you moved on and how you got personally comfortable with that." So, Mara met with him as his mini-mentor. No one had done it before, so no one could truthfully tell her she was doing it wrong.

Towards the end of that period, as Mara was preparing to go back to Genzyme, she had been doing a bit of consulting with a venture capital firm. There, she met Sue Segal, of Moore Holdings, LLC (maybe?). Sue mini-mentored Mara regarding the idea of changing her career path again. They discussed the idea of Mara running a small company instead of going back to Genzyme. Again, it was a challenge Mara could not resist. She took over a small company in California with a technology platform and moved it to Boston. Her new company had no biology, but Mara believed it was so powerful they needed to build their own proprietary content. She found a company in Boston called DNA Repair, focused on content with proprietary biomarkers to look for response to cancer therapies. Merging this content with her company's technology, she worked with MDV to form On-Q-ity.

The new company and CEO role is the a perfect culmination of all the experiences Mara has gained. She is able to assure the company has a crisper focus that is relevant to issues in health care today. As a result of the merger, Mara gained 19 employees in one day, which is very unusual for a start-up company. Many of these employees are women, and she works diligently to provide the appropriate amount of mentoring to both the women and men in her organization.

Due to her desire to lay new track and remain in a position of creating something, Mara is complex, not easy to mentor and not able to have only one mentor. She now has what she calls a suite of mentors on various issues rather than one mentor who knows everything. This approach gives her enough context to get the advice she needs.

Eunice Azzani

CEO, Azzani Search

Former Principle Partner, Korn-Ferry Executive Recruiting

Although she has spent 23 years with Korn-Ferry, Eunice's first career was as a librarian. She fell in love with information while working her way through college in the library. She had an epiphany of sorts in realizing that librarians weren't getting people the information they needed. So she decided to pursue a library science degree in college, but she quickly perceived that the big jobs in the library world were going to guys. She fought the battle for women in library leadership while in graduate school in her native Texas.

Eunice and her family moved to San Francisco from Texas where she promptly took a job as a legal secretary, because they had no money. She emphasizes that women should never be embarrassed to get and utilize a broad range of skill sets, so if she has to take a step back until the opportunity presents itself to move up, she can earn a living to help provide for her family.

Eunice had made the decision she wanted to work in the business world rather than in academia, because she wanted to move up the ladder faster. After about 18 months, she found a professional librarian job at Deloitte-Touche Consulting that launched her business career. She was there for five years when she received a call from Korn Ferry looking for someone with a master's degree in research and science to come run its research department. Although Eunice was leery of becoming a recruiter, her affinity for people drew her to the interview.

In addition, Eunice saw the opportunity to fulfill her desire to become a "big dog" at the top of an organization driving strategy and making major decisions about the company's direction. At Deloitte she would have to become a CPA to move up in leadership, and since she did not want to do that, she knew she would never achieve the desired status there.

Eunice has spent her entire recruiting career at Korn Ferry, recently moving on to form her own research firm. Labeling herself a "change junky," she continues to take interesting paths to get to what she wants to do.

Recruiting helped Eunice feed a driving passion for people and for helping great organizations hire great people. "Short of performing life-saving surgery, helping people find their life's work is one of most important things you can do. It really gives me a great deal of fulfillment, and I have been fortunate that it also gives me money.

Eunice says she recently "volunteered to be fired", because she was alarmed that the company was downsizing all young people. Although she just turned 60, she is quick to point out she did not retire, because, as she puts it, she is not a retiring kind of person. "We negotiated a good divorce, and I left to form my own search firm with my son and his wife," Eunice explained. "I always wanted to leave a family legacy, and personally, you don't feel you can control legacy with a big firm. Recruiting is still my professional passion, so it was never about the work, but about wanting to leave a legacy."

In the same vein as Mara Aspinalla, Eunice feels

more people should volunteer to leave a company, because we end up staying as long as we possibly can, and after you've stayed for a long time, you are so locked in that you lose site of external things. Her motto is, "If your baggage doesn't fit in the overhead bin, you need to go." She feels she should have left five years ago as it seems she has been through the same cycles four or five times. The other clue that she should have left sooner is that she has no regrets about leaving. It has worked out well for everyone. Korn Ferry still gives her firm searches, and she also sends clients their way.

There is something about taking a foray into entrepreneurship that is very freeing, according to Eunice. Initially she feels she was trying to mold Korn Ferry into what she wanted it to be for her legacy. But she now acknowledges this is something you have to figure out how to do on your own. She believes a big part of taking the plunge into entrepreneurship is timing and where you are in your life. Her dream is to spend the next five-to-eight years helping her son and daughter-in-law build the family business, and if they love it, they can carry it on.

On women in the workplace, Eunice has a lot of lessons to share. She has witnessed many women who tend to believe that if they just do really good work they will get what they deserve. Women are smart and capable, but don't understand there is more to success than just doing great work. "You don't get what you deserve, you get what you negotiate," Eunice cautions. She has seen many women solely focused on doing a good job. However, you have to realize that organizations are political. Therefore, you have to be strategic, political while managing your career and life within them. Learn to communicate with people and deal with them, understanding it is not all as clear cut as you might believe.

In Eunice's experience, men are much more political than women in organizations. For the most part, men are running things and tend to be drawn to taking care of other men within the organization.

Women also have to have a thicker skin. Eunice feels very fortunate in this area, because she was the only girl in a family of five siblings. Because her brothers put her through all kinds of situations, she had to learn how to stand toe-to-toe with them. Therefore, she had no trouble in the corporate world standing up, being counted, pushing back and not being intimidated if she wanted to participate. Even more importantly, it taught her to not take things personally. She realized early her ability to speak up and not just accept things. The upshot of her advice is that early intervention of dealing with men can be helpful for women maneuvering in the workplace.

Eunice shared a conversation with me about a woman she once shared a panel with. This woman landed a new role in her company with an office next door to the CEO. She began to have a stream of men coming in to meet with her with their "cry face" on, discussing their need for more money. No woman ever did it.

Women have not reached the place where they feel confident enough that they really have made it - even when they have. Unfortunately, we do not have a culture that recognizes women as leaders. Even women don't see women as leaders, and men don't see women as leaders.

Eunice's research during her Korn Ferry days showed this is one of the bigger issues facing women in the workplace. Although this is a major challenge, part of her feels strongly that women have to get comfortable in their own shoes, and in doing so, they will show up as a leader. If women can do this, it will matter more than anything else.

Eunice admits that sometimes it is hard for women, because they have not been able to play as much at the top level, and it's a leap of faith to get them there with their experience. Some companies may not have confidence in women leaders, but recognize that a place like this is not a place they want to be anyway. The bottom line is to know your stuff, and because there are a lot of people, you will have to deal with up and down the ladder.

Ask Mary

I recently relocated to the West Coast, and it seems to me people shut down when I come in the room and otherwise try to avoid me. How can I become part of the "inner

circle," so that I can move up the career ladder?

This is one of those questions I am frequently asked and have to kind of dissect before I respond. As I probe deeper to get more information before I give any advice, nine times out of 10, the person asking that question has some type of, for lack of a better word, flaw that is causing them problems. Many times she is a great worker, has strong potential, but is totally oblivious to the problem.

Eunice Azzani cites regional differences as a very real barrier for some people. "There is definitely a bias when your are working with organizations on both coasts. There is the sense that West Coast candidates don't work as hard, and East Coast candidates have too much of an edge and don't have sensitivity."

Feedback she has received about some East Coast candidates interviewing for West Coast jobs is that she is too "New York" (i.e. abrasive, insensitive, buries snide insults by adding a laugh on the end, as though that made the comments less insulting, and so forth.) The sad part is when she shared this information with some candidates, the response was disbelief and to brush it off with more incredulous, snide comments about whomever may have made the observation.

On the flip side, she has encountered candidates moving from California to New York and having difficult, because they are deemed too "California" (i.e., laid back, passive, not enough initiative, etc.) Eunice notes that all of these candidates are exceptionally bright and talented. But somehow, each sabotaged that talent and capability with personality glitches.

Yet there are people who work hard and do well on both coasts. I would urge you to seek some earnest feedback from your boss, peers and those who may work for you or support you to make sure there is not some flaw that is holding you back. If you do receive feedback that there is some type of "flaw," by all means do something to address it. Do not just brush it off as unimportant or irrelevant. It may not be a big deal for you, but it could be a showstopper for your staff or your company.

That said, it could also be a lack of certain skills or expertise. If that is the case, you need to get more training and/or education to shore up any necessary areas that will be required for you to successfully perform the desired job.

Talk to your boss about your goals and desires. Create a development plan that clearly outlines where you want to be in your career in one year, three years and five years, and share that with your boss. Ask your boss to honestly tell you if the opportunity to achieve those goals are possible in your current company. If the answer is no, ask someone else in human resources and/or in leadership – just to be sure you are getting an unbiased response.

Chapter Highlights

- Even the hardest working woman, who has prioritized and planned out every step of her family life, career and future aspirations, cannot make amends for "fatal flaws."

- Many bright and talented people with promising futures end up derailing their potential because of missteps or character flaws.

- A misstep or faux pas, an error in judgment or conduct, a bad or awkward step or a step in the wrong direction – however you define it--there are certainly pitfalls to watch out for that can derail your work, credibility and career.

- Women need to understand that they will never fit into the guy club. Women really just need to be seen as who they are, while also understanding they do fit into the big picture.

- Choose your words carefully. Sometimes less is more.

- Be careful of those who stick too close. They may be after your job.

- Own what you know, but steer clear of the rest. It is someone else's to own.

- Don't be a victim, and don't burn bridges. Be

strong, confident and make friends.

• Listen to the advice of those who can mentor you.

• Remember women, someone is not always waiting to hand you a promotion. You need to stand up and ask for it. Waiting in the wings won't ever get you the lead role.

CONCLUSION

Truly, we are living in one of the most opportune times for women - not only in Westernized societies, but globally. Whether you create a legacy through a career in the corporate world, in a profession or as an entrepreneur, you have within your grasp all the power you need to achieve your dreams.

You already know you can't do it alone. You need advice and counsel as well as education and experience. Within this book, the women profiled and I have told you what we would say if we had the opportunity to sit down with you personally to provide advice and counsel about utilizing your power, staying progressive and setting priorities. The Missing Mentor can help answer some of your questions, guide you in your journey and help you chart a path to success for yourself. Some of you will be fortunate to have access to formal and informal mentoring. Be prepared, so you can get the most out of it.

While having a personal mentor would be ideal, it is simply not a reality for the thousands of women flooding the marketplace. This book can be that surrogate mentor for you at all stages of your career and life. Now that you have read it, you also have the tools to make the most of any exposure you may get to women in leadership or entrepreneurship that you want to emulate.

You should never feel stuck or without resources again. The women profiled in this book and I have taken time to share our experiences with reinventing ourselves ideally, so you are able to successfully go through the many transitions you will face in life, whether you initiate them or not. As mentioned in Chapter Two, none of us can do everything we want to do at all times. We live our life in stages, and you will need to have a plan of action for each stage of your life. It is quite likely that in the early stages of your career you will get the guidance you need through reading and studying the career path of successful leaders. You should also not assume only the most senior leaders could help you. I have learned from people at every stage of my career – including people who I managed as well as peers and superiors. My best friend gave me some good advice years ago that I still treasure – "Don't ever get to the place where you think someone cannot tell you anything." In other words, you can learn something from everybody you encounter in life. Conduct your interactions in an attitude of mutual respect, so you can receive it.

Above all, don't be afraid to go out and seek what you need to keep moving forward. What would you do if you had no fear? Whatever is your answer, start there with preparing your road map. Reading this book is the next vice president, executive vice president, senator, doctor, congressperson, cabinet member, business owner, pastor, mayor, attorney, CEO, CFO, community leader, educator, wife, mother, author – you name it. And don't feel you have to limit yourself to one role on this list. In the introduction, I asked a list of questions to help you ascertain if you are a woman of power, progress and priorities. By now your answers to all of the questions should be either "yes" or "I'm working on it!"

One of my favorite quotes can be found on my Facebook page - "Lead, follow or get out of the way." No matter how much I have achieved in life I have noticed I am always juggling one of these positions. Frequently I am in a leadership position. Sometimes I am following others' lead, so that there is genuine collaboration and advancement for all involved – this includes at home as well as in the office. Sometimes I just need to get out of the way and let the experts do their thing. Following this philosophy has helped my work life and my home life be much more enjoyable and peaceful. I don't have to make all of the decisions all of the time. I can be just as fulfilled by valuing the decisions of others.

I introduced the concept of "learning dialogues" in Chapter Six on Lifelong Learning. This is a way of thinking about how we build relationships with others. Take advantage of your need to create a list of regular books, magazines and websites as reference materials for your career learning and development by sharing the list with others and setting up informal opportunities to get their feedback on the materials. Invite them to share their list with you and provide the same feedback. You can do this one-on-one or with a group of women, either in your neighborhood, at work or at church. It is a way to find much needed "girlfriend" time and achieve some of your development goals as well. "Learning dialogues" are excellent examples of peer-to-peer mentoring or mini-mentoring. You can supplement your own sessions with our online Learning Dialogues on TheMissingMentor.com.

As you have read throughout The Missing Mentor, your ability to deal with change and remain flexible will be the deciding factors in whether you can maximize and enjoy what the future brings or whether you go through it feeling like a victim. After reading our profiles and experiences, you should be encouraged that there is always a good opportunity in waiting, no matter what known or unforeseen change you may encounter. Development and change go hand in hand. It will be helpful to remember the definitions of both. Change – to grow, arise and then increase or progress to a more complex state. Develop – to change and become larger, stronger or more impressive, successful or advanced.

Progress is not always about being the next CEO of a company. But it is about continuing to advance and improve yourself where you are. When I graduated from the University of Louisiana with a degree in communications, I had no plans to be a senior vice president in a health care company. I just wanted to get a job in television or radio and accepted the first one that came my way - as a secretary. By the time I graduated from the University of Southern California with a master of health administration degree almost 20 years later, my plans and dreams had evolved way beyond my imagination as a young college graduate with little experience under my belt. Similarly, you may be a retail clerk or an MBA graduate. Just know your dreams will evolve. The key is to be alert and listening for the opportunities. Listen internally to yourself, so you understand your unlimited capacity, and listen externally, to others and the marketplace. You'll hear your destiny in both of these places. Then look for opportunities to help others do the same thing.

Conclusion

Made in the USA
San Bernardino, CA
16 January 2020